The Clash of Cultures

The Clash of Cultures

The Dark Path to Genocide

Gursimran Singh

Alive Book Publishing

Additional copies may be ordered from the publisher for educational,
business, promotional or premium use.
For information, contact ALIVE Book Publishing at:
alivebookpublishing.com, or call (925) 837-7303.

Book Design by Alex Johnson

ISBN 13
978-1-63132-173-3

Library of Congress Control Number: 2022915233

Library of Congress Cataloging-in-Publication Data
is available upon request.

First Edition

Published in the United States of America by ALIVE Book Publishing
an imprint of Advanced Publishing LLC
3200 A Danville Blvd., Suite 204, Alamo, California 94507
alivebookpublishing.com

PRINTED IN THE UNITED STATES OF AMERICA

10 9 8 7 6 5 4 3 2 1

Dedicated to the Sikhs
Never Forget 1984

Contents

Preface

Sikhism in a Global World

To the average Western reader, the terms "Sikh" and "Sikhism" are likely to be concepts clouded by a certain haze. Perhaps they have vaguely heard these terms mentioned in the news, or perhaps they have a friend or acquaintance from the faith who has shared something of his or her beliefs and culture. Maybe they have seen the rather unique architecture of a Gurdwara nestled into the landscape of their city or town, or have some awareness that the "Indian" or "Punjabi" turban is not quite the same as an Arab headdress. Whatever their level of familiarity, it is rather unlikely that they would feel confident in holding forth on the central tenets of the Sikh faith or the nature of what we might more broadly call "Sikh culture." They may even be completely unaware of the fact that Sikhism constitutes the world's fifth-largest religion, a global religion whose adherents reside not just in India, but in London, New York, San Francisco, Seattle, Toronto, Sydney, Brisbane, and many other places besides.

The intention of this book is, in part, to offer a window to such a reader into the principles, values, and historical consciousness that informs Sikh life. Of course, such an introduction can always only be partial. Each Sikh—like each Christian, Muslim, Hindu, Jew, or another person of faith—has a personalized relationship with their religion. It is this individuality that contributes to the richness and vitality of any community or tradition. Nevertheless, the very purpose of any faith or culture is to provide individuals with a shared vocabulary to relate to their fellow man: concepts, principles, modes of behavior, ritual activities, and common history. Indeed, even when two individuals from the same culture or social group disagree, they are likely to do so through references to shared values and concepts, historical references, and experiences. Thus, even if no book can provide a total window into the heart and mind of every Sikh, it can provide the reader with some of the vocabularies to embark on a deeper understanding of the Sikh lifeworld. It is in this spirit that this text offers up an image of the Sikh culture to the reader.

Of course, selecting a point of departure for any culture is a tricky subject. Should one begin with the rhythms of the hymns that comprise the *Guru Granth Sahib*, the Sikh scripture? Perhaps a description of Sikh influences in Indian pop music, or details of their food and style of dress, may be more enticing and relatable? Or, must we begin along a darker path, attempting to explain why it is that the most internationally newsworthy incident associated with Sikhs in the past four decades was their supposed responsibility for the bombing of Air India Flight 182 as it flew from Montreal to London in June of 1985?

It is the contrast between these lighter and darker images that informs the central dynamic this book places at the heart of Sikh culture: namely, the relationship between principles and sacrifice. However beautiful and enticing the more colorful aspects of Sikh culture may be, the fact remains that the enduring core of the Sikh experience has long been defined by the willingness to stand by principles of truth, respect, justice, and equality. It is the willingness to sacrifice for these principles—even in the face of malalignment and slander by powerful state actors, most notably the Indian government itself—that provides the foundation of Sikh historical consciousness and self-understanding. And, if the reader can be brought into some understanding of this relationship between principle and sacrifice, as well as the historical experiences that inform it, then they will have grasped one of the deep and substantive qualities of Sikh culture.

One of the core motivations that define the Sikh community's interactions with other cultures is the dynamic between the "progressive" and "static" civilizations. Lawrence Harrison and Samuel Huntington, in classifying various groups based on their core values, beliefs, and institutions, granted Sikhs, amongst Jews, Basques, and Mormons, significantly higher scores than nearly all third-world countries, which generally promote "static" values (Harrison 2000, 300). It is with this lens we can view the cultural conflicts between the Sikh faith and the Indian state. The progressive values that define the Sikh culture often clash with the values of the predominantly Hindu culture, leaving the Sikhs with two options: assimilation or annihilation. As history will show, the Sikh tendency to maintain a distinct identity led to the nearly complete annihilation of the community.

When Air India 182 exploded mid-flight in 1985, both the Indian and Canadian governments were quick to blame "Sikh separatists," a narrative that has largely endured to this day. And yet, when investigative journalists Zuhair Kashmeri and Brian McAndrew began to dig into the details behind this incident for their book *Soft Target* (1989), a rather different story began to emerge. It was revealed that when the Canadian Security Intelligence Service had chased the culprits of the plane bombing to the Indian embassy, they had only been met with political interference on the part of the Indian government. Within sixteen hours of the explosion, as Canadian police were just obtaining the passenger list stored in the airline's computer, the Globe and Mail newspaper had *already* received information from Surinder Malik, the Indian Consul General in Toronto, about the names of two Sikh fugitives to be regarded as suspects. Consul General Malik himself canceled seats for his wife and daughter on Flight 182 just days prior to the bombing. The picture that Kashmeri and McAndrew assemble paints a far more murky and sinister picture, appearing to implicate the Indian government itself in the bombing and "in a devious and ruthless operation to manipulate and destabilize Canada's Sikh population. The operation has been orchestrated by India's intelligence service and has left the Sikh community estranged from Canadian society" (Kashmeri & McAndrew 1989, v).

To the outside observer, such reports may seem far-fetched, even conspiratorial. To the average Sikh—particularly one acquainted with the macabre horrors, disinformation campaigns, and outright lies that accompanied the Indian state's genocidal campaign against the Sikhs on Indian soil less than a year before the bombing—the picture painted by Kashmeri and McAndrew rings far more true to life. It reveals a darker side to the colorful life under "the world's largest democracy," a country in which draconian national security laws, military action, and police torture have become commonplace tactics used—not only to silence Sikhs—but any minority group who dares to question the hierarchy of the status quo and the authoritarian dominance of upper-caste Hindu culture. In this sense, to have a window into the core of the Sikh culture and experience is to have a window into a side of Indian life, politics, and culture that few movie producers, tourist agents, or diplomats would like the world to see.

For most Sikhs, 1984 is a year etched into their psyche; either through direct experience or through the images of the violence that circulated in the wake of the Indian military's assault upon their holiest of shrines, the Golden Temple (Harmandir Sahib), or the gruesome anti-Sikh massacres that followed shortly thereafter. It serves as a chilling reminder of their tenuous position in contemporary Indian society; an event made all the more menacing by the fact that—unlike atrocities of the Yugoslav War or Rwandan genocide—the Indian government has largely succeeded in erasing the events of 1984 from international consciousness. Well before 9/11 in the United

States, India had already mastered the art of masking its atrocities in the supposed necessity of combating "secession" and "terrorism."

However, if 1984 constitutes a painful wound in Sikh memory, it is also an experience that is rendered through a long collective history of principle and sacrifice. In this sense, the impact of 1984 upon the Sikh community should not be considered solely a moment of paralyzing suffering and pain, but also as a paradigm of resilience; a moment that serves only as the most recent example of resolve in the face of tyranny, oppression, and hierarchy. In order to understand this resilience, it is necessary to understand how similar events have marked Sikh self-consciousness, and it is that fact which informs the structure of this book.

The first chapter focuses heavily on the Sikh culture through the lens of the institutions developed by the Sikh Gurus. Beginning at the faith's inception in 1500, we note key moments and actions taken by Sikh leaders in laying foundations of the community. In particular, we focus upon the radical break that Sikhism sought to create with the hierarchical caste structures of Hinduism; a break that has not only proved threatening to upper castes but also informed their attempts to construe Sikhism as nothing more than a subsect or off-shoot of the Hindu religion.

Chapter two focuses on how the principles and institutions laid down by the Gurus were maintained and strengthened by various Sikh political, religious, and military leaders. Thus, the second chapter addresses the critical periods in the 1700s, in which the Sikh community not only endured brutal repressions from the Mughal Empire but also succeeded in establishing its own political rule aimed at realizing the socio-political tenets of the faith.

Chapter three builds upon this by examining the sacrifices made by Sikhs in the name of independence from the British, as well as the position they found themselves in under the newly established Indian nation-state. In particular, we examine how the final form of the Indian constitution violated many of the promises made by national leaders to the Sikhs during the anti-colonial movement, and the tension this set up between an overweening, Hindu-dominated central government and the majority-Sikh population in the state of Punjab.

Chapter four continues in this vein, tracing tensions escalated between the Sikhs and the Indian state through the 1970s, as the latter steadfastly refuse to consider Sikh appeals for reform and increasingly sought to paint their demands in terms of "secessionist" and "terrorist" tendencies. It is the spiraling of this dynamic that not only laid the grounds for militaristic state action against the Sikh community but also the demonization of (and attacks upon) Sikhs by ordinary Hindus. Both of these forces would play an essential role in the genocidal campaign which was unleashed upon the Sikhs in 1984, the subject of Chapter five.

In the concluding chapter, we examine the aftermath of 1984 and the repression that the Indian state continued to exercise against the Sikhs in the years that followed. Far from arguing that the Sikh experience in India is unique, however, we also examine how the very same national security legislation, law enforcement methods, and political techniques have been deployed against other minorities. In contrast to the often-cited contrast between secular Indian nationalism under the Indian National Congress, and the repressive turn of India's Hindu nationalism, the picture that emerges is one of surprising continuity.

This picture—one of a clash between the hierarchical principles and norms that inform upper-caste Hindu culture and the culture and aspirations of minority groups—is one that can, to a certain extent, be understood through Samuel Huntington's model of a clash of civilizations. With the passing of the Cold

War era, Huntington argues, global politics has shifted as "alignments defined by ideology and superpower relations are giving way to alignments defined by culture and civilization" (Huntington 1996, 125). Indeed, in a Post-Cold-War world, culture is both a unifying and divisive force. Expanding upon this idea, we might say political conflicts which would have previously laid bare propositional or axiomatic disagreements are now increasingly laundered through the screen of the sensibilities, perceptions, and ethos which inform different ways of life; a screen that masks differences in principle through the murky lens of cultural difference. This book, in some senses, accepts Huntington's proposition, while also seeking to lay bare both the distortions which Indian propaganda has produced about Sikh culture, as well as the actual conflicts of principle and belief that underlie the continuing tensions between Sikhs and a Hindu dominated state.

CHAPTER 1

Origins of the Sikh Faith & Culture

Chapter 1

Origins of the Sikh Faith & Culture

The South Asian subcontinent into which Sikhism emerged in the early 15th century was a geographical landscape marked by incredible social, religious, and political complexity. Despite challenges from local leaders, such as the Hindu hill rajas, the Islamic Mughal Empire was ascending to the throne of the region. While Mughal dominance politically asserted the preeminence of Islam on the subcontinent, the caste structures of the Hindu majority remained the primary form of social structure, even across religious divides. Though "Hinduism" itself was not a single religion (it consisted of a variety of beliefs and deities), it continued to thrive, alongside Sufi saints whose mysticism bridged the gap between orthodox Hindu and Islamic sects, and popular forms of religious belief.

These facts are not merely of antiquarian interest. In order to understand the Sikh faith, ideology, and culture, it is necessary to understand the environment in which the faith was forged, and how the struggle to assert a new vision of political and social life for progress against the dominant structures of the period shaped the core beliefs of Sikhism today. As defined by Lawrence E. Harrison and Samuel P. Huntington, "'human progress' can be understood as a movement toward economic development and material well-being, socio-economic equity, and political democracy" (Harrison and Huntington 2000, xv). Culture plays a crucial role in the determination of economic and social prosperity and often influences the implementation of political institutions, such as democracy. And as Stace Lindsay argues, culture is a significant determinant of a nation's ability to prosper because culture shapes individuals' thoughts about risk, reward, and opportunity. Therefore, cultural values hold weight in the evolution of human progress because they shape the way individuals think and interact with the very concept of progress (Lindsay and Harrison 2000, 282). Cultural values form the principles around which economic activity is organized — and without economic activity, progress is impossible. Thus it is helpful to understand the Sikh culture through the lens of human progress, and how its values influence the community as a whole.

As former President of the Czech Republic Václav Havel observed, "Cultural conflicts are increasing and are more dangerous today than at any time in history" while the former President of the European Commission agreed, stating "future conflicts will be sparked by cultural factors rather than economics or ideology" (Huntington 1996, 28). Indeed, we see that many conflicts involving the Sikh community occur along cultural lines, rather than political or economic. However, culture is a difficult concept to deal with politically and emotionally. It is also particularly difficult to evaluate intellectually because there are problems with definition and measurement and because cause-and-effect relationships between culture and other variables like policies, institutions, and economic development run in both directions. In this book, we examine the vast cultural differences between the Sikhs and the current Hindu ruling majority that ultimately led to the Sikh genocide of 1984. For many present-day Sikhs, these sacrifices and struggles are part of a living history that is well remembered and often cited; a history that Sikhs, as minorities, continue to defend from Hindu majority groups who seek to incorporate the religion into their own. They are, moreover, only the first of a long series of sacrifices that Sikhs have made to stand by the principles of their faith.

This Sikh self-perception of distinction, of forging a new path through sacrifice, is important to emphasize from the outset. For many contemporary Hindus, Sikhism is often viewed as something of a subsect within their own unwieldy collage of beliefs. A common argument is that Sikhism is simply the militaristic branch of Hinduism, and an offshoot of the Kshatriya, or a governmental and martial caste. Similarly, some scholars even tend to view the faith through the lens of the other religions—Islam and Hinduism—as a kind of hybrid of the two. Such scholarly perspectives can be attributed to the complexity of the religious landscape in which Sikhism emerged; in which certain rituals and religious concepts overlap due to long histories of interaction. However, the classification of Sikhism as a part of Hinduism has clear political motivations in the present day, bolstering the numbers of the "Hindu majority" in "democratic" India.

Aside from introducing the reader to the Sikh faith and culture, the key contention of this chapter is that Sikhism did—and still does—assert a decisive break from the 15th century religious, social, and political structures that have preceded it. While the faith draws upon ideas and elements of the world in which it existed, its synthesis of these elements produced something radically new: a vision of social relationships, tolerance, and political ethics that resonate strongly with the values today asserted in the form of human rights, egalitarianism, religious freedom, and good governance. Given the legacy of this break, and the challenge it presented to the predominant social, cultural, and religious structures within South Asia, it is not a surprise that—even in the present day— Sikhism is often treated as a threat; a faith and people in need of being firmly and violently tamed by the elite of the status quo, and subordinated to dominant socio-culture and political structures.

This chapter begins by examining the origins of Sikhism in

the line of the Ten Gurus who established it. The Gurus were not only essential in laying down and elaborating core principles, practices, and institutions of the faith, but also for their willingness to stand firm for them in the face of political persecution from the Mughal Empire. Following, the basics of the Sikh code of conduct and the most pertinent Sikh institutions established by the Gurus themselves are discussed. Taken together, these principles and institutions laid down the core of the Sikh faith and culture, whose instantiation in the political form we will examine in Chapter 2.

Guru Nanak & the Origins of the Sikh Faith

The Sikh religion is one of the youngest religions in the world, founded around 1500 CE in the region of Punjab, which is today split between western India and eastern Pakistan. At the center of faith lie the Ten Gurus who laid down its principles and foundations; the first of these being Guru Nanak. Nanak was born into a Hindu family in 1469, and stories of his youth and adolescence are suggestive of a divinely inspired personality with a spirit of questioning and critical thought concerning the social practices and hierarchies entrenched in the world surrounding him. One particularly striking example of this spirit is to be found in the story of Nanak's coming of age ceremony; a Hindu ritual in which high caste individuals are bestowed with the *janeau* (sacred thread).

At the time, only Brahmins and Kshatriyas, the highest in the Hindu caste system, were permitted to wear the *janeau*, which had become something of a passport to education, marriage, and social status. As the Brahmin began to place the thread around Nanak's neck, Nanak stopped him, questioning its purpose. The Brahmin explained that the *janeau* was the basis of the Hindu religion, that without it a man would be nothing more than the lowest of castes. Upon hearing this, Nanak replied: "Make mercy thy cotton, contentment thy thread, continence its knot, truth its twist. That would make a *janeau* for the soul; if you have it, O Brahmin, then put it on me. It will not break, or become soiled, or be burned, or lost" (*Guru Granth Sahib* 471). At the young age of nine, in other words, Nanak had already begun to question the core principles of the Hindu faith, hinting at his future as the leader of a new religion, unlike any that had existed before.

As Nanak matured into adulthood, so did this inspiration of the spirit, eventually leading him not simply to question the social and religious traditions of the world surrounding him, but to reject them entirely. Thus, speaking of the religions that dominated the region at the time, the Gurus' attitudes are plainly stated: "Neither the Veda nor the Kateb knows the mystery [of God]." Similarly, the Muslim qazi, the Hindu pandit, and the ascetic yogi are critiqued: "The qazi utters lies and eats what is unclean; the brahman takes life and then goes off to bathe ceremoniously; the blind yogi does not know the way; all three are desolated" (*Guru Granth Sahib* 33).

It is, of course, undeniable that certain themes and similarities can be found between Nanak's message and those of other religious traditions. His emphasis on unity and fundamental equality of human beings—in contrast to polytheism and casteism of popular Hinduism—find resonances in the monotheism of Christianity and Islam, as well as certain branches of *yogic* philosophy. Similarly, Nanak's status as a *guru*, or teacher, derives from the vocabulary of the socio-cultural world in which he lived. However, as the first Guru of the Sikhs, Nanak did not seek merely to criticize the world surrounding him. Rather, as the quotes above suggest, he sought to clear the ground for a new path, a new community, one distinct from the traditions that surrounded him. Thus, as Joseph Davey Cunningham expresses in *A History of the Sikhs*

  it was reserved for Nanak [the first Sikh Guru] to perceive the

*true principles of reform and to lay those broad foundations
which enabled his successor Gobind [the 10th Sikh Guru] to fire
the minds of his countrymen with a new nationality and give a
practical effect to the doctrine that the lowest is equal with the
highest, in race as in creed, in political rights as in religious
hopes. (Singh 1978)*

At the core of this new faith, Guru Nanak emphasized
universality and freedom, principles which the subsequent nine
Gurus advocated and further developed. The new faith, he
determined, must give new life and add a new cultural
dimension to the world. Guru Nanak formalized the three core
pillars of Sikhism as:

1. Naam Japo: meditation of one universal God and the
recitation of God's Name
2. Kirat Karo: honest earning through hard work while
accepting all in life as God's gifts and blessings. Sikhs are to
live a life of decency, morality, and spirituality.
3. Vand Chakko: share the fruits of earnest living with the
less fortunate, irrespective of caste, creed, color, or gender.
The community is a vital component of the Sikh faith, and
the spirit of giving is central to the Sikh culture.

Even then at its conception, the Sikh faith was rooted in
principles of universal love and respect and a rejection of core
beliefs from other major religions like Hinduism and Islam.
From its origins, Sikhism championed defiance of the caste
system, rejection of clerical authority, and promotion of equality
between the genders. These principles find particularly eloquent
expression in the writing of the third Guru, Amar Das:

There were no divisions of caste or rank, no sectarian
antagonisms,
No idols nor temples, nor creeds of particular nations,

There were no clashing forms of prayer and worship,
Nor any to worship or pray.
There were no mullas or qazis or hadjis;
No Sufis and no disciples of the Sufis,
No proud Kings, nor their subjects,
Nor Masters either, nor slaves.
There did not exist either the cult based on adoring worship
of Vishnu,
Nor that based on Siva, the passive male,
And Sakti, the active female:
There was neither friendship nor sexual appetite;
God was both creditor and debtor then,
Such being His pleasure.
(*Guru Granth Sahib*, Ang 1035)

While many—including the Indian government—consider
Sikhism as a simple offshoot of Hinduism or even a mixture of
Islam and Hinduism, such allegations can be proven
categorically false simply by examining the base principles of
the Sikh faith. One of the most critical and distinctive aspects of
Hindu culture is its caste system—so thoroughly ingrained into
Indian society that it has persisted for thousands of years with
minimal changes. At its broadest level, society is conceived of as
structured by a four-fold hierarchy of Brahmins (priests) and
Kshatriyas (warriors), beneath whom lie the Vaishyas
(merchants) and Sudras (farmers and laborers). Each of these
broad categories is further subdivided into specific caste and
subcaste groups (Dumont 1970). Falling outside the four-fold
hierarchy entirely are the "untouchables," who were generally
treated worse than animals by those of higher castes, to the point
that in some regions even their shadows were considered evil.
Guru Nanak, emphasizing the equality of human beings,
nevertheless stated "Nanak seeks the company of the lowest of
the low class, the very lowest of the low. Why should he try to

compete with the great? In that place where the lowly are cared for-there, the Blessings of Your [God's] Glance of Grace rain down" (*Guru Granth Sahib* 15).

Unequal treatment of women in Hindu and Muslim societies was equally concerning to Guru Nanak. In births, males were viewed as superior to females, and women who birthed only females were viewed as inferior. Women were often not allowed to leave the house and were barred from education or labor. Often married off at young ages with little to no agency in their marriages, women were obligated to follow the traditional practice of *sati,* in which at her husband's funeral, a wife would throw herself on the pyre and be burnt alive. Guru Nanak condemned this practice as well, writing: "Why call her inferior? From her, kings are born" (*Guru Granth Sahib* 473).

It was these core principles of egalitarianism, respect, and the unity of God that Guru Nanak instilled not only in his followers but also propagated through his travels. Traveling thousands of miles on foot, he visited pilgrimage places of Hindus and Muslims in India, Pakistan, Bangladesh, Sri Lanka, Myanmar, Nepal, Tibet, Sikkim, and Bhutan, as well as far beyond to China, Afghanistan, Iran, Iraq, Arabia, Rome, and Africa. Professor Abdul Majid Khan sums up his personality as follows: "Nanak was a prophet of universal love, a light-house for the whole of humanity, a redeemer of all mankind. Indeed, there is nothing parochial, sectarian, or communal about his message. The task of emancipating human beings from the yoke of oppression, injustice, superstition, and falsehood was entrusted to Guru Nanak... by God the Almighty" (Tuli and Kumar 2015, 12).

Institutionalization of Sikhism

Following his passing, Guru Nanak was succeeded by nine subsequent Gurus who carried forward his mission and developed foundational institutions to solidify the community of the Sikhs. A core belief in Sikhism is that despite the Gurus' different physical bodies, the divine light inspiring them remains consistent. In essence, the Ten Gurus embody the same light as Nanak, which shines through in the body of each Guru. As members of such a spiritual lineage, each Guru sought to develop institutions that would further solidify both the message of Sikhism and the community built around it. These institutions would become the core of the new religion, further emphasizing its status as a faith, community, and culture distinct from that of its Hindu and Muslim contemporaries.

This drive was already evident in Guru Nanak's first successor, Guru Angad Dev, who formalized the institution of Langar, a free community kitchen where Sikhs and non-Sikhs alike may partake of meals together. The radical nature of such a practice in 16th century South Asia, where commensality (i.e. the sharing of food) was (and remains) central to rules concerning caste purity, cannot be overstated. This institution not only provides food to visitors but creates a sense of equality and fraternity across caste lines. Additionally, Guru Angad Dev officially established the alphabet of Gurmukhi, more commonly known as Punjabi. He took great interest in the education of the children by opening many schools for their instruction and thus greatly increased literacy in a time when the privilege of education was reserved for high caste Hindus.

Guru Amar Das, the third Guru, further strengthened the practice of Langar, directing his disciples, whether rich or poor, high-born or low-born (according to the Hindu caste system), to partake in their meals together. Guru Amar Das also introduced the Anand Karaj marriage ceremony for the Sikhs, replacing the Hindu ceremony of walking around a fire. He also completely abolished the custom of Sati amongst the Sikhs. The custom of Pardah, in which a woman was required to cover her face with a veil, was also done away with, and instead female education and equality were emphasized. Most importantly, as the Sikh community grew and followers began to break off into smaller ascetic groups, he established a system of religious administration to unify the Sikhs under the authority of the Guru.

Guru Ram Das, the fourth Guru, was notable for his efforts to expand the physical and social infrastructure of the Sikh community. He founded the critical Sikh city of Amritsar and started the construction of the famous Harminder Sahib, famously known in the West as the Golden Temple. With four doors on all sides, the structure indicates that God holds no partiality for any place, direction, or time. Additionally, Guru Ram Das invited scholars, poets, artisans, and craftsmen from all over the sub-continent to settle into the newly established city of Amritsar, transforming it into a cultural hub and bustling trade market.

The fifth Guru, Arjan Dev, provided two fundamentals to the faith: formalizing a scripture for the Sikhs and establishing a spiritual center. He compiled all the verses of his predecessors, the previous four Gurus, and himself, in a formal scripture (the Guru Granth Sahib) and completed constructing the Harmandir Sahib (Golden Temple). He also designed the four doors of the Golden Temple, proclaiming: "My faith is for the people of all castes and all creeds from whichever direction they come and to whichever direction they bow." However, what Guru Arjan Dev is most known for is his role as the first martyr of the Sikh faith. As Sikhism gained followers, Mughal Emperor Jahangir, recognizing the Gurus and their increasing political and social power, felt threatened by how Sikhism's views contrasted with Islamic values and the Hindu status-quo. Aided by Hindu revenue official Chandu Shah in the Mughal court, Jahangir ordered the execution of Guru Arjan Dev. Guru Arjan was made to sit on a burning metal plate while white-hot sand was poured on him; he was then submerged in the freezing water of the Ravi river. The martyrdom of the Guru permanently shifted the course of Sikhism—until this time, it had remained largely focused on the peaceful and spiritual path.

This event would have a profound influence on Guru Hargobind Sahib, the son and successor of Guru Arjan, best known for developing the Sikh concept of the "saint soldier." Guru Hargobind organized a small army, training the Sikhs in the means of warfare and strategy while explaining that constant, extreme non-violence and pacifism would only encourage evil. He himself carried two swords—one representing spiritual authority (known as Piri) and the other temporal authority (known as Miri)—to concretely symbolize the sovereignty of the Sikh community. He also built the Akal Takht, one of the most important institutions in Sikhism, in front of Harmandir Sahib (Golden Temple) to provide a space for discussing matters concerning the general public and the common citizen. Where the Harmandir Sahib was a spiritual and religious center, the Akal Takht represented the political seat of authority for the Sikhs. Throughout the time of his leadership, Guru Hargobind Sahib fought four defensive battles against the Mughal forces, significantly outnumbered in each one.

Having developed a strong, centralized army that had demonstrated its prowess against the ruling forces, the confidence of the Sikh community skyrocketed. The seventh Guru, Har Rai Ji, spent most of his life in devotional meditation and continued the task of building up the Sikh Nation initiated by his predecessor, Guru Hargobind. Guru Har Rai opened small hospitals that provided free healthcare and medicine to those in need. Despite not directly engaging in political or armed conflict with the Mughal Empire, Guru Har Rai maintained the large military force developed by Guru Hargobind Sahib.

The eighth leader of the Sikhs, Guru Har Krishan, was the youngest of the Gurus. Installed as Guru at the age of five, he primarily focused on reinforcing the faith's message of equality and compassion. To the Sikhs, he became a symbol of service, purity, and truth. In 1665, when a massive outbreak of cholera and smallpox ravaged Delhi, Guru Har Krishan gave his life while serving and healing the epidemic-stricken people in Delhi; many of whose suffering had been ignored due to their caste and social status. This sent a powerful message to the Sikh community encouraging service to the community during hard times. It is because of this motivation that Sikhs across the world responded quickly to the 2019 Coronavirus pandemic.

The ninth Guru, Tegh Bahadur, ascended to the guruship at a time when tyranny (for those belonging to non-Muslim communities) was at its peak under the Mughal ruler Aurungzeb. In a campaign to cleanse the empire, Aurungzeb began forcing non-Muslims to convert to Islam. Amidst the chaos and persecution, a group of Hindu Brahmins approached Guru Tegh Bahadur and pleaded for their safety and security. The Guru then proceeded to confront Aurangzeb, declaring that if Aurungzeb could convince the Guru to embrace Islam, the Hindus would follow suit. Following extensive attempts at bribery, harassment, threats, and torture, Guru Tegh Bahadur, became the second Guru-martyr of the Sikh religion, sacrificing his life in defense of a religion that ran contrary to his own. Through this action the Guru demonstrated the commitment of the Sikh faith to religious freedom, becoming a paragon for sacrifices made not just in the name of the community, but for a broader concept of justice.

Guru Gobind Singh, the tenth and final human Guru, solidified the militaristic personality of the Sikhs, encouraging a culture resistant to tyranny, discrimination, and oppression. In 1699 AD, during an event known as Vaisakhi, the Guru gathered the Sikhs from throughout India in the city of Anandpur. From amongst the crowd, he selected five Sikhs from different castes and regions, who later became known as the "Panj Pyare" (the five beloved ones). Baptizing the five Sikhs first, then requesting their blessings to baptize him, the Guru became both the leader and the disciple of the Sikh nation, naming all initiated Sikhs as the "Khalsa." From this critical point, the Khalsa became a formidable force throughout India, ultimately shaping Punjab, along with the Northern region of the subcontinent.

One crucial aspect of the Sikh identity bestowed by the tenth Guru was a common last name for all baptized Sikhs. At the time, despite the rising popularity of Sikhism and the long-established nature of Islamic rule, the Hindu caste system was integral in daily society. As described by historian Perry Anderson:

Hindu social organization fissured the population into some five thousand jatis, few with any uniform status or definition across the country. No other system of inequality, dividing not simply, as in most cases, noble from commoner, rich from the poor, trader from farmer, learned from unlettered, but the clean from the unclean, the seeable from the unseeable, the wretched from the abject, the abject from the subhuman, has ever been so extreme, and so hardwired with religious force into human expectation. (Anderson 2013, 97)

It is not unexpected then, that the Sikh Gurus, who had long denounced the caste system and its divisive applications, would seek to solidify Sikhism's core values that ran against the grain of the generally accepted social hierarchy. In 1699, at the same baptizing of the Panj Pyare, Gobind Singh declared that henceforth, all men would adopt the last name "Singh," a Sanskrit word translating to "lion," and women would take on the name "Kaur," the Sanskrit word for "prince" or "royal". Prior to Guru Gobind Singh's declaration, these names and titles were generally reserved for the royal and upper castes. In a time when surnames were descriptors of caste and profession, the Sikh adoption of "Singh" and "Kaur" represented a rejection of the Hindu social order that had become so interwoven into society, and made it clear that the Sikh community sought to break the confines of the hierarchical system.

After Guru Gobind Singh, the position of the Guru was passed onto the Guru Granth Sahib, the current scripture of the Sikhs. Compiled, written, and edited by Guru Gobind Singh himself, the Granth, written in the Gurmukhi script, contains the hymns uttered by Guru Nanak and his successors, along with dozens of contributors from other faiths. It is regarded as the supreme spiritual authority within the community and held in great reverence by the Sikhs. It is also the only scripture of its kind that not only contains the writing of its own religious founders but also the writings of people of other faiths.

Once the Guru Granth Sahib was permanently installed, Sikh leaders began seeking to solidify a Sikh presence in the area. Establishing their own kingdom under the command of Sikh general Baba Banda Singh Bahadur, the Khalsa permanently etched their mark in Indian history; though short-lived, this reign galvanized and instilled confidence in the Sikhs. Following Banda Singh's reign, the Sikh community was once again thrown into a state of chaos and terror by Afghan invaders, who waged their own war of repression and extermination, cutting the Sikh population down to a fraction of what it had originally been. However, with the rise of Maharaja Ranjit Singh in 1799, the Khalsa established a second empire extending up to Tibet in the north and Sindh in the south, becoming one of the most powerful kingdoms in Asia.

Summarizing the distinctness of the Sikh religion's origins in his book *A History of the Sikhs,* historian Joseph Davey Cunningham stated:

> So Nanak [the first Guru] disengaged his little society of worshippers from Hindu idolatry and Muslim superstition and placed them free on a broad basis of religious and moral purity; Amar Das [the third Guru] preserved the infant community from declining into a set of asceticists; Arjun [the fifth Guru] gave his increasing followers a written rule of conduct and a

civil organization. Hargobind [the sixth Guru] added the use of arms and military system and Gobind Singh [the tenth Guru] bestowed upon them a distinct political existence and inspired them with the desire of being socially free and nationally independent. (Cunningham 1966 [1849], 80)

The principles instilled within the Sikh religion and culture made it radically progressive, both at the time of its founding and by today's standards. Indeed, the core concepts of respect, equality, charity, justice, and tolerance are difficult to find so prominently in any culture.

Sikh Code of Conduct

There is, perhaps, no better example of the progressive core of Sikh values than the approach taken to conduct in warfare; a domain of human activity whose violent seductions easily corrupt the principles of individuals. While Sikhs are well-known as militaristic and were viewed as a "martial race" by the British for this reason, the Sikh faith places a strong emphasis on principled conduct in violence and warfare. The founders of the Sikh faith instructed their followers in the basics of martial arts, known as *gatka*, not only for the purpose of self-defense but the protection of others in need; this was particularly pertinent in a time of tyranny and upheaval for the Sikhs as Mughals cemented their regime within the Indian subcontinent. Guru Gobind Singh, the tenth Guru, maintained this position, establishing a formal army fighting to resist the repressions of the Mughal regime. In his Zafarnama (letter of victory) to Emperor Aurangzeb, Guru Gobind Singh states "when all methods fail, then it is righteous to take up the sword" (Singh 2011, 23). In Sikh culture, in other words, it is not only a right but a moral obligation for each Sikh to oppose injustice and oppression by force only when other means have failed. It is crucial to note that while the Sikh Gurus encouraged resistance against tyranny, they also set strict codes to prevent abuse of power and infringement of human dignity.

The earliest recording of fully developed Sikh laws of war can be traced to the time of Guru Gobind Singh. These codes included orders for the humane treatment of prisoners of war, the injured, the surrendered, the slain, and non-combatants. Gobind Singh specifically forbade attacks on a fleeing enemy. During the First Sikh empire, in a battle against the King of Kahlur circa 1711 CE, the Sikh commander Banda Singh Bahadur ordered his soldiers "not [to] pursue a retreating soldier". Even in the heat of battle, Guru Gobind Singh encouraged the medical treatment of injured enemy soldiers, even organizing a volunteer medical task force for this purpose.

In his magnum opus known as the *Suraj Prakash*, Bhai Santokh Singh, an accomplished poet and historian, refers to a written code of conduct for Sikhs participating in war under the name *gurshastra*. He specifically refers to one of its provisions— that women were not to be molested under any circumstances. As a measure particularly relevant to the wartime in the 18th century, members of the Guru's army were explicitly forbidden from engaging in intercourse with Muslim women, as the Muslim Mughals were the main opponents. While today, this requirement seems an evident provision, it was a novel idea at the time. As Santokh Singh records the conversation between the Sikhs and Guru Gobind Singh:

All the Sikhs assembled together to ask the source of all values. Their question was: "the Turks routinely rape women [of India]. Sikhs would be doing well to avenge this. Why does the Guru's code (gurshastra) prohibit molestation of women?" Then, at that time, the True Guru spoke thus: "I want the Sikh community to scale (new moral) heights. I will not condemn it to depths of degradation." (Singh 1994)

Ratan Singh Bhangu, a Sikh historian during the late 18th century, mentions that Banda Singh Bahadur, appointed commander-in-chief of the Sikh forces by the Guru, used to repeat his general orders on the battlefield by the beat of drums every day. One order that was repeated daily was, "nobody is to touch ornaments on the person of a woman. Similarly, no man is to be divested of the clothes worn by him. More particularly, a person's turban was not to be removed" (Bhangu & Singh 1993, 166). In this context, one cannot help but note that it was only in 1949, following World War II, that the international community updated the Geneva Convention to include, among other things the stipulation that "Women shall be especially protected against any attack on their honor, in particular against rape, enforced prostitution, or any form of indecent assault" (1949 Geneva Convention, Article 27). In this regard, the Sikh community can be seen as well ahead of the times. Despite warring with the tyrannical Mughal regime that often harassed non-combatants, the history of Sikh warfare is conspicuously lacking in incidents involving attacks on civilians.

These principles can be observed in action right down to the present day, in which Sikhs continue to form an essential backbone of the Indian army. During the 1971 Bangladesh Liberation War, in which the Indian government asserted itself militarily in support of Bangladesh's independence from Pakistan, the Sikh soldiers of the Indian army came upon countless victims of genocidal rape, in which over 200,000 Bengali Hindu and Muslim women were systematically identified, raped, and killed. Often, these women were kept as sex slaves, dirty and naked, for Yahya Khan's (the President of Pakistan) army (Saikia 2011, 152-170; Mookherjee 2015, 159). It is recorded that the Sikh soldiers of the invading victorious army, in a befitting tribute to human dignity, removed their own turbans to cover the naked women. Incidents such as this testify to the enduring strength which the tenth Guru's *gurshastra* has maintained as a fundamental aspect of Sikh culture.

Another aspect of the Sikh war codes was the prohibition of

any attack on places considered holy by any group of people. Despite repeated assaults on Sikh shrines by the Mughal and Afghan armies, including the destruction of the holiest Sikh site in Amritsar, the Sikh army never retaliated in kind. Even during the destruction of the provincial Mughal capital of Sirhind, the Sikhs did not touch the tomb of Sheikh Ahmed, an implacable tyrant and nemesis of the Sikh community, who was nevertheless respected by Muslims throughout the empire. The extent of his regard can be judged by the fact that Sheikh Ahmed, responsible for the execution of two Gurus and two of Guru Gobind Singh's children (aged 7 and 9 respectively), was buried alongside several princes of Afghanistan. Despite his inhumane actions and active oppression of the Sikh community, Sheikh Ahmed's tomb was not desecrated by the Sikh army of Banda Singh Bahadur in any way. While the city of Sirhind was itself razed, the mausoleum of Shaikh Ahmed and other significant Muslim princes remains standing to this day.

Sikh Institutions

By the beginning of the eighteenth century, the Sikh Gurus had succeeded in firmly establishing a faith, community, and culture. However, as Daniel Etounga-Manguelle notes, "culture is the mother; institutions are the children," and thus the Gurus also concretely laid down strong foundations for the culture, at the core of which was a set of institutions that acted to maintain and reproduce the principles upon which the faith was founded (Etounga-Manguelle and Harrison 2000, xxviii). These practices, organizations, rituals, traditions, and places act to solidify the Gurus' teachings and provide resources for the community to collaborate, learn, and engage in discourse.

The most essential institutions of the Sikh faith are:

1. **The 5 K's:** The 5 K's are articles of faith mandated for all initiated Sikhs ("Khalsa" or "Amritdhari") by Guru Gobind Singh at the creation of the Khalsa in 1699. Forming the external identity of a Sikh, the 5 K's can be understood as a type of uniform, through which any Sikh is recognizable.

    a. Kesh - Long, uncut hair, or "Kesh," is the primary marker of an Amritdhari, and is considered inseparable from the Sikh. A baptized Sikh is to never cut or trim their hair, so as to maintain their distinctive appearance. In a world where short, trimmed, hair is the norm, Sikhism encourages its followers to stand apart with the kesh.

    b. Kara - The "Kara" is an iron bracelet worn around the wrist, typically the right, constantly reminding a Sikh of their actions. It is also a symbol of a permanent bond to the community, and a link in the chain of the Khalsa.

    c. Kanga - A small wooden comb worn in the hair, and serving as a marker of cleanliness, the "Kanga" serves an important purpose daily in a Sikh's life. At the time of the Khalsa's founding, holy men often allowed their hair to become tangled and dirty; the Guru commanded his Sikhs to remain both spiritual and clean.

    d. Kachera - The "Kachera" is a type of basic undergarment worn by all baptized Sikhs as a commitment to readiness and a willingness to be ready at a moment's notice. Further, it allowed the Sikh soldier to operate in combat freely and without hindrance or restriction because it was easy to fabricate, wash and carry compared to other traditional under-garments of that era, like the dhoti. The Kachera also symbolizes self-respect, reminding the wearer to maintain control over lust.

    e. Kirpan - The "Kirpan" is a dagger symbolizing a Sikh's duty to defend those in danger, and is only used in self-defense or the defense of others. Much as a police officer is expected to wear a side-arm when on duty, a Sikh is to wear the Kirpan at all times, and it serves as a constant reminder to stand for justice and righteousness.

2. The Gurdwara: Hinduism has its temples; Buddhism its stupas; Christianity its churches and Islam its mosques. For the Sikhs, Gurdwaras serve as auditoriums, forums, classrooms, temples, and places for the congregation to sing hymns. Here, the devotion of the congregation and the connection among the people is considered to be of greater importance than any monetary contribution. Gurdwaras can generally be classified into two categories: "historic" and "communal." "Historic" Gurdwaras are associated with the Gurus and act as markers for significant events. For example, Harmandir Sahib (Golden Temple) was created by the fifth Guru; Nankana Sahib marks the birthplace of the first Guru; Sis Ganj Sahib indicates the location of the Ninth Guru's martyrdom. "Communal" Gurdwaras are constructed anywhere there is a need; i.e. in any village, town, or city with a Sikh population. Thus, these centers serve to bring together the local community and encourage the upkeep of the Sikh morals and values. "Gurdwara" literally means "the house of the Guru," and it is, therefore, a sanctum sanctorum for the Sikhs that serves as material actualization of their devotion, communal bonds, and respect. Although all Gurdwaras are marked by these qualities, one among these holds particular importance.

Harmandir Sahib (Golden Temple): One of the most famous and holy sites in the Sikh religion, the Harmandir Sahib, was constructed by the Fifth Guru. It can be compared to the Mecca of the Muslims, Jerusalem of Jews, or the Vatican of the Christians, but it is vastly more. Along with the Akal Takht, situated across from the Harmandir Sahib, it is the capital of the Sikh spiritual and political world. Despite having been destroyed multiple times by the Mughal government and various Mughal invaders, the Harmandir Sahib was always rebuilt. In 1809, following another destruction of the temple, Maharaja Ranjit Singh restored the Harmandir Sahib plated with copper and gold. As Sirdar Kapur Singh wrote:

When the Sikhs do not have a sovereign state of their own, the Golden Temple, with its surrounding complex, continuously retains its theo-political status, which may be suppressed by political power, compromised by individuals or questioned by politicians, but which remains and never can be extinguished, for, it is sui generis and inalienable, and imprescriptible. It is owing to this unique status, grounded in certain peculiar doctrines of Sikhism that, many misunderstandings continuously arise concerning the use of the Golden Temple with its surrounding complex, for Political purposes', for allowing ingress into it and housing of those whom the political state may deem as 'offenders', and for pursuing, 'extra religious activities' from inside its precincts. The Sikhs, themselves, have never viewed any of these activities, started or controlled from inside the precincts of the Golden Temple, as either improper, or repugnant to the Sikh doctrine, or contrary to the Sikh historical tradition. (Singh 2016)

3. Akal Takht: Following the martyrdom of his father and the Fifth Guru, the Sixth Guru, Hargobind Sahib Ji, took up arms for the defense of the innocent. To further solidify this institution, Guru Hargobind constructed the Akal Takht (Throne of the Timeless One), a seat of political power directly across from the Harmandir Sahib. Here, the Guru administered justice among the Sikhs and issued orders. He employed bards to sing ballads of heroism. Whereas the Harmandir Sahib was the house of religion, the Akal Takht was the house of political authority. Today, the Akal Takht represents the fundamental institution of political independence, emphasizing the idea that the Sikh community is not beholden to any one nation or government. Gurbachan Singh Nayyer says: "During the middle years of the 18th century, the Akal Takht served as the most important center of the political activity of the Khalsa" (Pettigrew 1995, 37).

4. Langar: The fundamental institution of Langar, the practice of providing communal free meals, was started by the very first Guru and maintained by the following Gurus. It aimed to remove the distinctions between castes and creed, which were pervasive in the predominantly Hindu culture at the time. In a Langar, everyone sits together and is fed the same food—referencing the fundamental ideas of equality and giving back to the community. The donation of a portion of one's own earnings and time in the service of humanity is heavily encouraged. Highlighting the importance of Langar, the Tenth Guru stated "There is nothing equal to the bestowal of food. Blest is the man who giveth to the really hungry. Let no one fix a time for the exercise of this virtue. It is not necessary to consider whether it is night or day, evening or morning, whether the moon is dark or full, or if there is a particular anniversary. Nor is it necessary to consider what the social position of the applicant may be. Avoid all delay in such a matter. Charity is of all gifts the greatest, for it saveth life". (Macauliffe 1909, 105) This institution of Langar applies the teachings of Sikhism—particularly service and equality—to the real world. To this day, every Gurdwara serves Langar to all regardless of background. However, the concept of Langar is not limited to the Sikh Gurdwaras: local and international Sikh organizations provide aid in war-torn and disaster zones, continuing the tradition of Langar.

5. Sarbat Khalsa: Every six months, the Sikh community is to meet in a deliberative assembly, along the same lines as a

Parliament. Literally translating to "entire Sikh Nation," the Sarbat Khalsa served to bring together the Sikhs to voice their concerns and address political differences. Amidst a sea of various authoritarian and tyrannical regimes, the Gurus and their Sikhs thus established a form of direct democracy. The Gurus were clear that the Sikhs were never to violate principles of human dignity, and that all people, regardless of religion, political background, race, color, or ethnicity were granted the same rights of independence and sovereignty. The first Sarbat Khalsa was held by the tenth Guru himself in 1708 before his passing and continued regularly during the periods of Sikh rule. At that time, Sarbat Khalsas were held twice yearly, at Vaisakhi and Diwali. In 1986, over two hundred thousand attended the Sarbat Khalsa, coming from all parts of Punjab and representing many of its organizations and villages.

6. Martyrdom: Tying together all of these institutions is the concept of sacrifice and martyrdom, a principle that establishes the weight and force behind all other Sikh institutions. Indeed, it was only through such dedication that the Sikh community was able to survive in the turbulent world into which it was born. In this regard, Sikhism departs from the rest of the Indic religions and cultures. Traditionally, Indian religions and cultures promote asceticism and pacifism, but the Gurus state that one is to live a life of commitment to the cause of love, and in the pursuit of it, one must inherently struggle against oppression. In this, the Gurus led by example, with the Fifth and the Ninth Gurus giving their lives in defense of not only their own but the religion of others as well. For centuries during and after the time of the Gurus, Sikhs have repeatedly given their lives for the causes of justice and in opposition to oppression. Unlike Islam, a religious tradition with a comparatively prominent tradition of martyrdom, Sikhs who die in pursuit of justice do not look forward to eternal life in paradise. Though some elements of heavenly aspiration have undoubtedly crept into Sikh popular culture, on the whole, and in its original form, sacrifice is a tradition focused on this one life. G.S. Mansukhani, who wrote a popular primer on Sikhism, stated that "those who know the art of true living also know that of true dying" (Mahmood 1997, 196). This perfectly encapsulates the Sikh understanding of death. Sikhs perceive themselves as always in control of their own destinies, even in the face of death, that one thing that overcomes any human attempt to control; sacrifice and martyrdom represent the liberation of utter control over fate, ultimately placing faith in God. While minor aspects of the institution have shifted over time, martyrdom and sacrifice have been thoroughly ingrained into the Sikh religion and remain a fundamental aspect of the culture today.

CHAPTER 2

The Sikh Empire

Chapter 2

The Sikh Empire

With the passing of the tenth Guru and the appointment of the Granth Sahib, the history of Sikhism entered a new epoch. The divine light which had inspired Gurus was now passed on to and firmly embodied in scripture, principles, and institutions. For future generations, the task was now to carry this spiritual and cultural patrimony forward, and to ensure its realization in the shifting social, political, and economic situations of their times. Framed in the terms of German sociologist Max Weber (2013, 212-54), the charismatic authority of individual Gurus had now been routinized into the authority of a tradition.

However, as this chapter shows, ensuring the survival and growth of this tradition was no easy task. For both Sikh leaders and adherents in the 18th century, the central question was how this new faith, and the radical departure it represented from the norms and social hierarchies of medieval South Asian society, would relate to political power. As we have already seen in the previous chapter, the relationship between Sikhism and the hegemon power of the Indian subcontinent, the Mughal Empire, had been fraught from the very beginning. While the tensions began with the very first Mughal emperor, Babur, conflict truly escalated during the reign of Emperor Jahangir, the fourth Mughal ruler, who tortured and executed the fifth Guru, Arjan Dev. Similarly, the ninth Guru was beheaded for his defiance of the Mughal campaign to forcibly convert the Hindus. Under nearly every Mughal ruler, Sikhism was perceived as a threat to imperial authority, religious dominance, and the existing socio-political order, and though the Sikhs had endured multiple atrocities since the inception of the faith, the 18th century marked a particularly harsh period in the faith's history. Mughal persecution solidified Sikh resolve, brutally demonstrating the fact that if Sikhism was to survive, it could not do so under the oppressive thumb of Mughal rule. This reality reinforced Sikhism's strict ethical code and tendency to promote sacrifice and righteousness over life.

The events of the 18th century in northern India thus mark a critical turning point in the Sikh community's experience. Under the Guru Granth Sahib, general Banda Singh Bahadur's command over the Khalsa army kept the Sikh forces united against the threat of the Mughal empire. At the time, Hindus, Sikhs, and other religious groups were persecuted under the Islamic regime as governors imposed strict jizya taxes (fees levied on non-Muslim subjects). Hindu hill rajas largely remained aloof and uninvolved beyond their own districts; though at times they would aid the Mughal empire, leaving the Sikhs to challenge the combined Islamic and Hindu forces. Under Banda Singh, however, the organization of the Sikhs eventually came to bear fruit—at least in the Punjab region—as the Sikhs triumphed over an oppressive Mughal regime.

Banda Singh's reign, though short-lived, demonstrated the Sikh capability to rule, permanently boosted the morale of the community, and provided a blueprint for the integration of Sikh institutions into Sikh governance. The social and political impacts of Banda Singh's rule in 1710 were arguably more influential than the ideals of the French Revolution in 1789 as he promoted a more egalitarian system that starkly contrasted with the hierarchical system of the Mughals. By the end of the 18th century, Banda Singh's successes would be built upon by Ranjit Singh, who would succeed in establishing a Sikh Empire that remained one of the most progressive governments in the history of South Asia. Following the establishment of the core

Sikh principles and institutions by the ten Sikh Gurus, it fell on the political leaders of the faith to enact these foundational beliefs into practice; the Sikh periods of rule represented the implementation of those institutions that had proven so critical to the maintenance of the Sikh community.

Moreover, unlike the regimes that preceded it, the Sikh Empire was based on the core principle of "prosperity for all," violating the norm of the zero-sum social model that had dominated the Mughal and Hindu reigns prior. Beyond those responsible for genocidal campaigns and mass killings of Sikhs, few Muslims or Hindus were mistreated; in this aspect, the Sikh rule remains distinct in its lack of harassment of other communities within the empire. Civilians were not outright targeted nor were the religious buildings of other groups razed—both common practices at the time. Common citizens were not looted, nor were women captured, raped, or sold into slavery. Indeed, the Sikh rule can be defined as a revolutionary period that broke the mold of economic and social development in the region, a fact largely attributable to the core principles laid down in the Sikh faith and institutions. Even before the Enlightenment in Europe, which advocated ideals like liberty, progress, tolerance, and fraternity, we find evidence that the Sikh religion, and later, the Sikh Empire, had already endorsed and implemented such "revolutionary" ideas.

Banda Singh Bahadur & the First Sikh Empire

Banda Singh is one of the most well-known warriors and leaders in Sikh history, having established the first Sikh rule in the Indian subcontinent. Born on October 27, 1670, under the name of Lachman Das, Banda Singh's journey to Sikhism was rather unique. At the age of 15, Lachman Das left home to become a Hindu ascetic, changing his name to Madho Das and establishing his own monastery. In 1708, Guru Gobind Singh visited Madho Das, at which point Madho Das became his disciple and was initiated with the new name of "Banda Singh Bahadur." As a blessing for future battles to come, Gobind Singh gifted Banda five arrows.

Shortly after the Guru's assassination later in 1708, Banda Singh assumed command of the Khalsa forces, assuming both political and military leadership of the Sikh community. Banda Singh moved quickly to establish independent Sikh rule through the capture of the provincial Mughal city of Samana, where he ordered the minting of new coins to establish the sovereignty of the Khalsa and provide a financial foundation for the budding empire. Within a year, Sikh forces controlled territory from the Sutlej River to the Jamuna River (Sagoo 2001, 128). This dramatic expansion surprised the long-standing Mughal Empire, heralding the decline of that empire's centralized authority in the face of regional powers. With the ability to wield sovereign authority, Sikh political and military leaders sought to implement the Gurus' principles through new policies and methods of statecraft.

In keeping with the Gurus' teachings of equality and the rejection of oppressive authority, Banda Singh Bahadur halted the zamindari system in 1710 (Jawandha 2010, 81). Established under the Mughal empire, the zamindari system was analogous to the feudal system of Medieval Europe, extracting wealth from the peasantry through a capricious system of taxation and funneling it to the Brahmin and Kshatriya upper castes, who constituted the religious and political elite. With the abolition of the system, Banda Singh redistributed land among the farmers, thereby establishing a more equitable and rationalized system of administration. Reforms such as these not only advanced economic prosperity but also fostered the development of a more prosperous agrarian class that stabilized, at least partially, the turbulent unease in the region. Perhaps even more importantly for the Sikh community itself, Banda Singh's reign demonstrated the capacity of the Sikhs to rule with the compassion found in the principles of the Gurus, which instilled a fire of confidence within the community. Though short-lived, the first Sikh rule shifted the political and military dynamic of the northern subcontinent. In the declining years (namely, from 1715 to 1716) of his rule, the Mughal army captured Banda Singh, parading him in a cage through the streets alongside 780 Sikh prisoners in chains, 2000 Sikh heads mounted on spears, and 700 cartloads containing the heads of slaughtered Sikhs in order to instill fear and terrorize the common population. Describing the scene, one Muslim source notes:

On this day I had gone to see the spectacle as far as the salt market and thence accompanied the procession to the Imperial Fort. There was hardly anyone in the city who had not come out to see the [spectacle] or to enjoy the show of the extirpation of the accused ones. Such a crowd in the bazaars and lanes had been rarely seen. And the Musalman could [not] contain themselves for joy. But those unfortunate Sikhs, who had been reduced to this last extremity, were quite happy and contented with their fate; not the slightest sign of dejection or humility was seen on their faces. In fact, most of them, as they passed along on their camels, seemed happy and cheerful, joyfully singing the sacred hymns of their scripture. And if anyone from amongst those in the lanes and bazaars called out to them that their own excesses had reduced them to that condition, they quickly retorted saying that it had been so willed by the Almighty and that their capture and misfortune was in accordance with His Will. And, if anyone said, "Now you will be killed," they shouted, "Kill us. When were we afraid of death? Had we been afraid of it, would we have fought so many battles with you? It was merely through starvation or want of food that we fell into your hands, otherwise you already know what deeds we are capable of." (Singh et al. 1935, 220)

At the Imperial Red Fort in Delhi, the Sikhs were imprisoned, starved, and abused. Every day one hundred Sikh soldiers were brought out of the fort and publicly executed. After the soldiers had been killed, Banda Singh himself was brought out along with his four-year-old son, Ajai Singh. Refusing when ordered to kill his own son, Banda Singh's son was then murdered in front of him, his heart cut out, and thrust into his father's mouth. At this point, even Persian sources noted Banda Singh's resolve as his eyes were gouged out, his limbs severed, and his skin removed from his body (Singh et al. 1935, 233-34). While Banda Singh's reputation as a warrior for the common people and the first to establish a semblance of a Sikh kingdom marks him as one of Sikhism's most inspirational figures, his solidification of the central tenets and institutions of faith, and his willingness to sacrifice his life for them, inspired the Sikhs to continue to fight oppression and rebuild.

Mughal Persecution

Following the fall of the first Sikh empire, the Mughals, eager to re-establish their hold on the northern Indian region and ensure the Sikhs did not rise once again, began numerous reprisal campaigns aimed at eradicating the Sikh faith. Sikhism and the Mughal dynasty both took root within the same time frame; consequently, much of the Sikh struggle through the lifetimes of the Ten Gurus, centered around resistance to oppression and tyranny.

In 1716, Mughal Emperor Farrukh Siyar, in an attempt to eradicate the entirety of the community, ordered that all Sikhs were to convert to Islam or accept death. With rewards offered for, quite literally, the head of each Sikh, hundreds were kidnapped from their villages and publicly executed. Even following the death of Farrukh Siyar in 1719, large Sikh festivals and temples were attacked. His successors offered substantial bounties for information regarding the whereabouts of any Sikh, implementing blanket rewards for those who brought back the skulls or distinctive hair of Sikhs. The looting of Sikh homes and businesses was made lawful—even encouraged—and those who dared to withhold information or shelter the Sikhs were liable to be executed (Singh 1978, 127).

To prevent access to the Harmandir Sahib and Akal Takht—two of the most important shrines and institutions to the Sikhs—a military occupation was initiated and the complex was defiled with the consumption of drugs, prostitution, and alcohol on its premises. Despite this, the Sikh community endured, though its numbers were quickly dwindling. Then governor of Lahore Zakaria Khan asked in frustration, "I have debarred them from all occupations. They realize no taxes, they do not farm, nor are they allowed to do business or join public employment. I have stopped all offerings to their Gurdwaras [temples]. No provisions or supplies are accessible to them. Why do they not die of sheer starvation?" (Singh 1998, 325) Where Banda Singh had solidified the institutions of the Gurus, the Mughal emperors that followed the fall of the Sikh empire sought to uproot the same institutions. The 5 K's, critical to a Sikh's distinct physical appearance, were targeted, forcing many to either abandon their faith or hide in dense jungles. Gurdwaras, most prominently the Harmandir Sahib and Akal Takht—along with the institution of Langar—were demolished and defiled. Sarbat Khalsas were unfeasible, as large groups of Sikhs were easily discovered and eliminated; the Sikh community was fractured and quickly diminishing. Although Mughal actions against the Sikhs during the 18th century were wide-ranging, two events, in particular, left an indelible mark on the community's collective memory.

Genocide I (Chhota Ghallughara) - 1746

In June of 1746, the first of two Ghallugharas—a word that

can be roughly translated as "massacre" (though there is no direct equivalent)—took place as the Hindu minister Lakhpat Rai, serving under the Mughal Empire, under the authorization of Lahore governor Yahiya Khan (son of the infamous Zakaria Khan), mobilized an army tasked with eliminating "infidels;" its first action being the rounding up and execution of the Sikhs of Lahore. From there, the army set out for the forests roughly 80 miles to the northeast of the city, where Sikhs were known to be living in hiding, and began a systematic search for anyone in the jungle. Heavily outnumbered and woefully under-equipped, the Sikhs residing in this area attempted to escape to the foothills of the Himalayas to the north. As they crossed the river Ravi, coming within sight of the foothills, the Sikhs were greeted by the armies of the Hindu hill chiefs, allied (at least in this instance) with the Mughals. Completely encircled by the hill chiefs and the Mughal forces, the Sikh band found itself in desperate circumstances.

After heavy and desperate fighting, the Sikhs managed to break through the encompassing armies, once again crossing the river Ravi in an attempt to find sanctuary in another forest 150 miles to the south. Exhausted and beset by enemy forces, many lost their lives in the river's strong current. An estimated 7000 Sikhs were killed and 3000 captured during this operation. The prisoners were marched back to Lahore, paraded in the streets, and publicly executed. Given the already dwindling number of Sikhs at the time, the losses during this event were incredibly devastating. As a result, this event became known as the "Chhota Ghallughara," the first genocide. At this time, the Harmandir Sahib and Akal Takht remained occupied by the Mughal forces. Lakhpat Rai went on to order all Sikh places of worship be destroyed and the scriptures burnt, decreeing that anyone uttering the word "Guru" be put to death, even outlawing the Punjabi term for sugar [gur], which sounded similar to "Guru" (Nijjar 1995, 460-61).

Following the disastrous Chhota Ghallughara, as Sikh places of worship were destroyed and desecrated, thousands of Sikh men, women, and children were tortured and publicly beheaded. According to historian Nur Ahmed Chishti, the governor of Lahore ordered 1100 Sikhs to be executed at the horse market in celebration of Eid. Additionally, special military units were created and specifically tasked with the hunting of Sikhs while mercenaries capitalized on the high rewards for Sikh civilians. According to one eyewitness, "They ran after [the Sikhs] up to 67 kilometers (42 mi) a day and slew them wherever [the Sikhs] stood up to oppose them. Anybody who brought a Sikh head received a reward of ten rupees per head" (Singh, Singh, and Sidhu 1997, 467). The same account also reported that "the Sikhs who were captured alive were sent to hell by being beaten with wooden mallets. At times, Adina Beg Khan [a Mughal administrator] sent 40 to 50 Sikh captives… they were as a rule killed with the strokes of wooden hammers" (ibid). Sikh women and children were explicitly tortured and used for slave labor, starved, and forced to grind grain in prisons. According to a Sikh account, "Many of the women were given merciless lashings, working all day exhausted from thirst and hunger, they plied their stone-mills… as their children, hungry and thirsty, wailed and writhed on the ground for a morsel, the helpless prisoners… could do little except solace them with their affection until, wearied from crying, the hungry children would go to sleep" (Seetal 1971, 271). Even as power changed hands between different Mughal regimes, the policies towards the Sikh community remained tyrannical, as they were hunted, tortured, and executed. This continuity can be observed in the fact even sixteen years after the first "small" genocide of 1746, the Sikhs would suffer an even more spectacular loss. As a result, the Sikh culture was ingrained with a sense of constant resistance and struggle against state-sponsored violence, which even continues in modern-day India.

Genocide II (Vadda Ghallughara) - 1762

While the general persecution under Mughal rule spelled an ill fate for the Sikhs, the mid-1700s brought their own troubles, compounded by the invasion of neighboring Afghan rulers into the Gangetic plains. In the eighteen years following the Chhota Ghallughara, the Punjab region suffered five invasions, several years of rebellions, and civil wars. Under these circumstances, it was unprofitable and infeasible for any authority to thoroughly execute a campaign of oppression against the Sikhs; indeed at times the Sikhs were often sought and valued as useful allies in the various power struggles. However, once even temporary peace was restored, the governor of Lahore, Shah Nawaz, and his Afghan allies continued their campaigns of repression.

The second of the two Ghallugharas took place in February of 1762, perpetrated by the Afghan invader Ahmed Shah Durrani and a new Mughal governor of Lahore, Mir Mannu. In a surprise attack on a large caravan of Sikhs numbering about 30,000, the majority of whom were not soldiers, Durrani's forces harassed the procession, killing and capturing wherever possible. A secondhand account by the son and nephew of two eyewitnesses described the scene: "Fighting while moving and moving while fighting, they kept the baggage train marching, covering it as a hen covers its chicks under its wings" (Bhatia 1998, 396). More than once, the troops of the invader broke the cordon and mercilessly butchered the women, children, and elderly inside, but each time the Sikhs regrouped and managed to push back the attackers. Following two days of heavy fighting, the forces went their separate ways, with an estimated 10,000 to 20,000 Sikhs killed and hundreds more dragged back to Lahore in chains (Singh and Rai 2008, 76). Durrani then headed for the Golden Temple and struck in April 1762, at a time when thousands had gathered for Vaisakhi celebrations. The Harmandir Sahib, which had been previously destroyed and rebuilt a mere five years before, was blown apart with gunpowder, while the surrounding pool was filled with the debris of destroyed buildings, human bodies, and animal carcasses. As a crowning desecration, a pyramid of Sikh heads was erected. Once again, a significant portion of the total Sikh population was annihilated, threatening the very existence of the community (Singh and Jyoti 2008, 77).

Within a few months of the first attack on the Harmandir Sahib, the grandfather of Maharaja Ranjit Singh, a future Sikh ruler, managed to temporarily wrest back control and rebuild the Gurdwara, only to lose it when Durrani returned the next year. Once again, the Golden Temple was defiled and destroyed. However, swift military action on the part of the Sikhs allowed them to annex Lahore and declare their sovereignty over the whole of Punjab. The persecution of the Sikh community did not come to an end until the creation of the sovereign Sikh Empire under Ranjit Singh, who built forts along the famous Khyber Pass to prevent any further invasions from Afghanistan. Much like Banda Singh, the Sikhs minted coins and declared Lahore a seat of authority to cement their political power in the region.

Maharaja Ranjit Singh & The Second Sikh Empire

While Banda Singh's reign was short-lived, his leadership and the blueprint he provided for practical implementations of Sikh institutions inspired future political and military leaders— most notably Maharaja Ranjit Singh. Almost 80 years after Banda Singh's death and a period of turbulence and political infighting, Maharaja Ranjit Singh would manage to establish a Sikh empire more expansive and lasting than Banda Singh's rule. This kingdom—which stretched throughout the Punjab region from the Khyber Pass in the west to Tibet in the east, and from

Kashmir in the north to Sindh in the south—would endure from 1799 to its annexation by the British in 1849.

Much like Banda Singh before him, Ranjit Singh's rule was notable for three key features: (1) the promotion of religious tolerance, (2) efforts to further equality, and (3) principles of rational governance. To be sure, these three qualities can be found in varying degrees in different kingdoms and empires throughout South Asian history—even, in some contexts, under the Mughal Empire that sought so brutally to exterminate the Sikh faith. Yet Ranjit Singh's rule remains notable in the *degree* to which it embodied these characteristics, an impulse that finds its roots in the principles of Sikhism and its institutions. In short, much like Banda Singh before him, Ranjit Singh sought to actualize the core values of Sikhism in governmental form, in the process developing a variety of policies that, in the secular terms of the British rulers that followed them, would be called "good governance."

The tolerance of Ranjit Singh's regime was perhaps its most noble quality, a fact all the more notable given the suffering that the community had endured for almost two centuries at the hands of the Mughals. Despite the Sikhs only making up 6% of the empire's population, from its very inception, Ranjit Singh sought to differentiate his government from the forms of repression and reprisal which characterized early periods. As historian Patwant Singh notes, "[Ranjit Singh's] first action on occupying Lahore was to issue an order that all his officers and troops were to treat people of the city with courtesy and consideration... He rode through Lahore's streets to assure citizens of their personal safety and the safety of their property to leave no doubt in their minds that they would be safe under his rule" (Singh and Rai 2008, 100). Among testimonies of Ranjit Singh's generosity towards his foes can be cited from Major H.M.L Lawrence, a political agent in charge of British relations with Lahore during Ranjit Singh's rule: "While those of the royal blood are all but begging their bread in Delhi and Kabul, he [Ranjit Singh] almost invariably provides for the families of his conquered enemies" (Lawrence 1970, 30-31).

This attitude of tolerance continued even after Sikh power was well-established and assured. Individuals were allowed to rise to high governmental positions irrespective of caste or religion, and through the empire's territories, orders were issued to treat people in accordance with their faith, thus guaranteeing religious freedom (Singh and Kohli 1986, 56). At the general level, people of different castes, creeds, and religions were encouraged to assemble together to celebrate religious holidays and promote brotherhood. Likewise, the military was fully integrated, promoting camaraderie amongst Hindus, Muslims, and Sikhs alike (Roy 2011, 143-147). As the appointment of key posts was based on merit and loyalty, the government was run by an elite corps drawn from a variety of communities, giving the Sikh governance a kind of secular character, even as it derived its core values from the Sikh faith (Duggal 201, 125-126). It is perhaps for these reasons that, in paying tribute to the Sikh empire, the British colonial officer, Baron Charles Hügel states "never was so large an empire founded by a man with so little criminality" (Hugel and Jervis 1845, 382).

These principles of tolerance were supplemented by a concern for equitable governance and social equality, a fact that can be readily observed in the importance that Ranjit Singh— like Banda Singh before him—attributed to education. Indeed, according to British Historian G.W. Leitner, Punjab was one of the most educated places in the world during the Sikh empire of the Maharaja (Verma 2021). Despite lacking formal education himself, as education was restricted by caste prior to his rule, Ranjit Singh sought to use education as a means to elevate the quality of life for his people. The British East India Company, after a survey, discovered that education in Lahore and Punjab was "far superior to the education the British had introduced all over conquered India" (Verma 2021). In Lahore alone, there were 18 formal schools for girls, including specialist schools for technical training, languages, mathematics, and religions, which included Hinduism, Islam, and Sikhism. There were craft schools specializing in miniature painting, sketching, drafting, architecture, and calligraphy. "The East India Company concluded that the Punjabis were years ahead in the field of education than the so-called 'enlightened' Europeans. Every village of Punjab provided education, which was compulsory for females; thus, every woman was literate, oftentimes even more educated than men" (Verma 2021). As a result, as Dr. Leitner observes, the literacy rate of the Sikh Empire increased annually.

A similar attention to social equality, as well as the principles of rational and efficient administration, can be found in the justice system established under Ranjit Singh. Building upon local judicial bodies, the system promoted efficient justice, while also integrating checks against abuse of authority. Under this system, the local village body dealt with crimes, thefts, murders, disputes, as well as all civil or criminal misdemeanors. However, "the victim or accused could appeal if unsatisfied with the verdict or even file a written appeal to the Maharaja himself. Ranjit Singh would sometimes ask for reports on certain judgments. There was no capital punishment in the land" (Singh and Rai 2008, 181).

Ranjit Singh's concern for rational and effective governance can also be observed in his effort to promote security, trade, and stewardship of natural resources. Charles Baron von Hügel, an Austrian diplomat, described Ranjit Singh as a trailblazer in this effort to ensure the safety of traders in Kashmir, stating:

Before Ranjit Singh took possession of the valley, her trade routes were not safe and the costly shawls were often looted en route by the robbers. The Maharaja made special arrangements to safeguard the goods of the traders… In case of any loss of goods in transit, the traders were compensated. The trade routes were made safe to the extent that highway robberies became a thing of the past... The longest trade route was from Lahore to Petersburg via Kashmir. (Hugel and Sharma 1984, iv)

Similarly, writing on the subject of resource management in 1844, Lieutenant Willaim Barr, notes that in Ranjit Singh's Punjab: "Wood, strange to say, is not to be bought, nor could I ever get sufficient for a small frame... However, on asking the Maharaja's officers about it, they told me... Ranjit Singh would not allow a tree to be felled until it is actually required for use" (Barr 1844, 65).

Taken together, these three dimensions of the Maharaj's rule—tolerance, equality, and rationality—merge together to form an overall picture of the kind of culture and society that Ranjit Singh sought to cultivate within his empire. Ranjit Singh was fully aware of the importance of making every citizen in his realm feel an integral part of—and entitled to—the best that his rule had to offer. It was critical for the well-being of the state that its people should develop a sense of fellow feeling and religious tolerance. Simultaneously, this state could only provide for its populace to the extent that it was efficient and effective in guaranteeing justice and economic well-being. Aside from the typical interest of any ruler in guaranteeing general security, Ranjit Singh proved particularly forward-thinking in the role which he accorded not only simply to education, but to education that any person—male or female; rich or poor–could access.

A prosperous, generous, and compassionate kingdom founded on the principles of Sikhism, Ranjit Singh's reign can serve as a testament to the progressive nature of the Sikh religion and culture. In Patwant Singh's words, "His passion for ensuring just governance for his people, his dedication to secular beliefs, his respect for God-given life and the uncompromising stand against tyranny enjoined by the Sikh Gurus—these were articles of faith from which he seldom deviated" (Singh and Rai 2008, 109). The Sikh culture, derived from the Sikh religion and the teaching of the 11 Sikh Gurus, fundamentally promotes respect and integrity for other religions and cultures, even those that directly oppose the Sikh faith. The Sikh war codes of conduct, established centuries before the Geneva Convention, implemented strict regulations to protect all non-combatants regardless of their affiliation with any group or party. It is notable that keeping with the "sarbat tha bhalla" (welfare for all) slogan encourages and compels Sikhs to seek the well-being of everyone in the world. Where the Gurus had clearly laid out the tenets of the Sikh faith, Ranjit Singh successfully institutionalized the Sikh faith and its core principles in his kingdom.

Although the task of government in any setting or period is beset by numerous difficulties, it is thus not without reason that many Sikhs take a great deal of pride in the accomplishment of Ranjit Singh and his empire. This is true not simply because he sought to institutionalize the core values of Sikhism–tolerance, egalitarianism, brotherhood–into the form of a state, but also because of the broader example this state set for any ruler or politician truly dedicated to public service. Indeed, it is a model that might well continue to provide lessons to governments of the present day, and one that the Sikhs present to the world when championing an independent Sikh nation.

CHAPTER 3

Sikhism at Indian Independence

Chapter 3

Sikhism at Indian Independence

Given its breadth, the concept of "culture" can often take on the paradoxical quality of being both powerful and deterministic, as well as elusive, pliable, and open-ended. Thus, in the work of political scientists such as Samuel Huntington (1996), "culture" assumes the role of an *independent* variable that provides a causal explanation for global conflicts. Some anthropological renditions are even more extreme, arguing that culture (particularly language) determines the nature of reality itself, as we are able to perceive and understand it (Saphir 1929). By contrast, other scholars have approached culture as a *dependent* variable, suggesting that it is essentially a product of the institutions, power relations, or the force of charismatic personalities (Althusser 2001; Gramsci 1971; Weber 2013, 212-54). A reasonable approach, it seems, must strike a balance between the two. In the preceding chapters, for example, we have witnessed the importance of the culture and institutions developed by the Gurus and the strengthening of those values by leaders such as Banda Singh Bahadur and Ranjit Singh. Once established, these elements of the faith have been propagated forward in time not just by the inertial authority of "tradition" (Weber 2013, 226-41), but also by the dedication and sacrifice of the Sikh community to uphold and defend them.

As we have already observed in the preceding pages, many of the core tenets of Sikh culture emerged as an explicit rejection of Hindu culture and social structure: human equality vs. caste hierarchy, monotheism vs. polytheism, and so forth. Thus, even as Sikhs such as Guru Tegh Bahadur sought to defend the right of Hindus to religious freedom under the Mughals, they did so from a position of confidence in their own principles and identity. When India won her independence in 1947, however, it almost seemed as though roles had been reversed. Under a democratic system in which demographic weight determined political power, the Sikhs now found themselves confronted by a "Hindu majority" that, while ill-defined and riven with caste, class, and regional conflicts, nevertheless asserted itself with increasing confidence. This new majority began to assert its power against the Sikhs in two contradictory ways: assimilation and annihilation. Regarding the latter, Cynthia Keppley Mahmood states, "The absorption of previous religious heterodoxies such as Buddhism into the Hindu system has provided a model for modern Hindu expectations of non-Hindu religions, and has served as a negative example for those intent on retaining a separate religious identity, such as Sikhs" (Mahmood 1989, 326). Indeed, as Mahmood suggests, Hindu dominant culture and religion has historically attempted to "absorb" other cultures and religions—one example of which can be drawn from the fate of the Buddhist culture in India, which was enfolded into the Hindu culture, as the shrine of Bodh Gaya, the site of the Buddha's enlightenment, became a Hindu temple for centuries. However, the Sikhs have resisted similar attempts at absorption and annihilation, largely due to the nature of the Sikh culture cultivated by the Sikh Gurus and institutions like the Akal Takht, which emphasized the importance of the sovereignty of the community. In the modern era, the Sikh culture has essentially been placed under siege, trapped between a rock and a hard place: to assimilate or to be annihilated.

In this chapter, we will examine the form that attempts at assimilation took at Indian Independence, particularly in the drafting of the Constitution. As we shall see, the ultimate form of this document and subsequent legislation broke many of the promises which Indian leaders had extended to the Sikhs during the nationalist movement. As would be expected of a community that had resisted centuries of Mughal persecution, the Sikhs refused to quietly submit to their absorption into the Hindu fold and remained steadfast in their demands and petitions for recognition of their identity and autonomy. In the chapters that follow, we will examine how the Indian state, and ostensibly secular Hindu politicians, reacted when it became clear that Sikhs would not meekly submit.

Nation-State or State-Nation?

Following World War II, in 1947, a militarily and economically crippled Britain ended its 200-year colonial occupation of the Indian subcontinent following decades of protests, boycotts, and rebellions as part of the Indian independence movement. Prior to colonialism within India, there had never been a thorough concept of the "Indian nation," only a general opposition to the British occupation and a vague notion of a collective identity. Upon the liberation of India, the constitutional document entailing the freedoms and governmental structures of the nation stated that India would be a "sovereign socialist secular democratic republic," promising justice, liberty, and equality for all. Yet, in living up to these ideals the founders of India faced a serious challenge: there was no singular idea of India. Citizens could belong to the Indian territorial State, but ultimately also expressed their pride as Hindus, Tamils, Sikhs, and Muslims.

States tend to be tied to territory, establishing clear borders that are recognized by other countries, while nations are a group of people who identify as a cohesive collective based on shared cultural or historical values. In some ways, nations can be thought of as "imagined communities" (Anderson 2016) bound together by notions of unity that can be predicated on religion, ethnic, or cultural identity, often ignoring political boundaries to the extent that a nation may overlap between multiple states. In their book *Crafting State-Nations: India and other Multinational Democracies* (2012), political scientists Alfred Stepan, Juan Linz, and Yogendra Yadav argue that ethnically diverse societies like India have one of two options when attempting to balance the objectives of nation-building and democracy-building.

One path established is the construction of a nation-state, in which the political boundaries of the State reflect the cultural boundaries of the nation. States often attempt to form homogenous nations within their geographic and political borders through symbols, education, patriotism, and national interests. Nation-states develop a constitutional document for the safety and security of the nation, not necessarily for the protection of individual citizens. Thus historian Eugen Weber describes how French leaders, in the wake of the French Revolution, transformed "peasants into Frenchmen" by championing a common cultural, linguistic, and national identity that was uniquely French (Weber 2007). When cultural homogeneity is prioritized within a nation-state, minority groups may find their cultures slowly extinguished through assimilation, disposed from economic or political opportunities if they refuse to integrate into a hegemonic national culture, or — in the worst cases — forced to emigrate or targetted in genocides.

However, for societies that already possess strong cultural diversity, at least some of which are territorially based and supported by identities not strictly tied to the nation, the nation-state model is often ineffective at best and counterproductive at worst. In these cases, Linz, Stepan, and Yadav provide an alternate proposal — the state-nation. While a nation-state commands the alignment between the boundaries of the State and nation, the state-nation allows for a multitude of communities to coexist under the umbrella of a broader democratic system, recognizing that citizens tend to have multiple, overlapping identities that need not detract from a larger sense of national unity.

Is India a "nation-state" or a "state-nation"? This is a dilemma that the Constituent Assembly (the collection of founding delegates of India) grappled with when drafting the Constitution. In many respects, the founders sought to build what might be considered a state-nation model. For example, the borders of the individual union territories of India were drawn based on the differences in language. Moreover, under Article 29 of the new Constitution, citizens "having a distinct language, script, or culture... shall have the right to conserve the same." Freedom of religion was supposedly guaranteed under Article 25, and a system of reservations (similar to affirmative action) was established in an attempt to guarantee lower caste groups opportunities in political, economic, and educational life.

All of these designs, however, were the subject of hard-fought political battles between the leaders of the Indian nationalist movement. Gandhi and Ambedkar clashed over the issue of whether lower castes should be granted "separate electorates" in which they—and they alone—would vote and elect representatives to government bodies. Similarly, provisions—such as the "special status" of Kashmir—were made to ensure that regions or groups with highly distinctive identities would remain integrated into the fledgling states. In other words, questions concerning what form the new Indian state would take, and how much it would embody something like a "state-nation" model, were not idealistically pondered in a vacuum. Rather, they were the subject of intense power struggles and political debate; a debate that was in part responsible for the bloody Partitioning of British India into independent India and Pakistan.

Within these debates, sacrifices that Sikhs had laid down for the independence movement formed the cornerstone of their demands for recognition within independent India. In the 1860s at the start of the independence movement, the Sikhs composed less than 1.5% of the total population. Nevertheless, their disproportionate willingness to lay down their lives for this cause is well evidenced:

1. 77% of those hanged and 81% of those sentenced to life imprisonment were Sikhs.

2. During the Quit India Movement, led by Mahatma Gandhi, Sikhs comprised 70% of the total Punjabis arrested.

3. Of the 20,000 soldiers who immediately volunteered for the Indian National Army, 60% were Sikhs.

4. As a result of the Partition of August 1947, 40% of the entire Sikh population was made refugees.

In recognition of the disproportionate sacrifices made by the Sikh community, India's founding fathers solemnly pledged that the Sikhs would be granted autonomy over their region and that their dignity would be safeguarded. One prominent founder (to become the first Prime Minister of India), regarded as a hero by a vast majority of the population and a self-purported secularist, Jawaharlal Nehru, on July 6th, 1946, declared that the "brave Sikhs of Punjab are entitled to special consideration. I see nothing wrong in an area set up in the north of India wherein the Sikhs can also experience the glow of freedom" (Dhillon 1974, 376). Similarly, Gandhi pledged to the Sikhs at the time:

> I ask you to accept my word... and the resolution of the Congress that it will not betray a single individual, much less a community... Our Sikh friends have no reason to fear that it would betray them, for, the moment it does so, the Congress would not only thereby seal its doom but that of the country too. Moreover, the Sikhs are brave people. They know how to safeguard their rights by exercise of arms if it should ever come to that. (Mahmood 1997, 113)

From the very outset of Indian Independence, however, the bold promises and aspirations which the nationalist movement had held out to the Sikhs were dashed. Unable to reconcile the representational demands of Muhammad Ali Jinnah's Muslim League with those of Nehru and Gandhi's Indian National Congress, the British elected to bifurcate the "crown jewel" of their empire into two: Pakistan created as a putative Muslim homeland and India as Hindu majority state (Bose & Jalal 2018, 130-158). The confused and arbitrary nature of this decision led to both mass migrations, and mass violence, as many Muslims in India fled across the border to Pakistan, while Sikhs and Hindus in Pakistan migrated toward India.

Immediately, one of the greatest migrations in human history began, as millions of Muslims trekked to West and East Pakistan (the latter now known as Bangladesh) while millions of Hindus and Sikhs headed in the opposite direction. Hundreds of thousands never made it to their final destinations. Across the Indian subcontinent, communities that had coexisted for almost a millennium attacked each other in a terrifying outbreak of sectarian violence, with Hindus and Sikhs on one side and Muslims on the other—a mutual genocide as unexpected as it was unprecedented. Nisid Hajari, in *Midnight's Furies* (Houghton Mifflin Harcourt), writes of the Partition:

> *Gangs of killers set whole villages aflame, hacking to death men and children and the aged while carrying off young women to be raped. Some British soldiers and journalists who had witnessed the Nazi death camps claimed Partition's brutalities were worse: pregnant women had their breasts cut off and babies hacked out of their bellies; infants were found literally roasted on spits. (Hajari 2016, 5)*

What followed, especially in Punjab, the principal center of the violence, was one of the great human tragedies of the twentieth century. Hajari continues, "Foot caravans of destitute refugees fleeing the violence stretched for 50 miles and more. As the peasants trudged along wearily, mounted guerrillas burst out of the tall crops that lined the road and culled them like sheep. Special refugee trains, filled to bursting when they set out, suffered repeated ambushes along the way. All too often they crossed the border in funereal silence, blood seeping from under their carriage doors" (ibid). In this way, nearly two million people were killed (Perkins, n.d.). What was meant to be a graceful triumph following nearly a century of colonial oppression became an unprecedented massacre and bloodshed. In the previous chapters, we have seen the guidance provided by the Sikh institutions and reigns of Maharaja Ranjit Singh and Banda Singh in effect during the Chhota Ghallughara and Vadda Ghallughara. However, during the Indian Partition, after 98 years under oppressive British colonialism, even Sikhs (for the first time in such a capacity) joined in on the attacks on innocents, demonstrating a clear degradation of the core Sikh institutions. "The darkened landscape bore silent witness to trains laden with the dead, decapitated bodies, limbs strewn along the sides of roads, and wanton rape and pillaging" (ibid). As the Punjab and Bengal were essentially split in half, nearly seven million Hindus and Sikhs and seven million Muslims found themselves on the wrong side of the border, and the clashes that resulted occurred primarily along religious and cultural lines.

For the extreme violence that occurred during Partition, one could blame the hastily drawn borders created by the British, who created all the borders of South Asia within five weeks. One could point to the increasingly hostile rhetoric that accompanied the rise of Hindu and Muslim nationalism or the divide and conquer strategies employed by the British during their colonial period. The popularly accepted narrative of Partition stresses these factors and characterizes the violence as neighbor turned against neighbor, with bands of armed men stirred into madness.

For the Sikhs, however, this division did more than claim lives and properties, for the new western border did not just divide "India" from "Pakistan," but also split the Punjab region into two, a region in which the vast majority of Sikhs resided. Consequently, in joining the Indian state, the Sikhs were forced to leave behind nearly 200 shrines in a soon-to-be hostile state, several of which are located in the very birthplace of the founder of Sikhism, Guru Nanak. Punjab was divided, prioritizing the needs of what would become India and Pakistan, but the lingering effect has been one of a communalized and fractured Punjabi identity. Muslim Punjab identifies closely with Pakistan, while Indian Punjab is split between the Sikh and Hindu cultures. Sikh and Punjabi identities have become synonymous since the political movement to set Punjabi as the official language of the state. Hindu Punjab largely identifies with the Hindutva project. As a result of Partition, Punjabis as an ethnic group have been divided and sub-divided along religious and linguistic lines. The Punjabi language is now almost exclusively associated with the Sikh community, despite having served as the mother tongue for Hindus, Muslims, and Sikhs throughout northern India. It is difficult to think of another region in the sub-continent that has shunned its own linguistic and ethnic history in favor of a national or religious identity in such a way; the majority of Indian states, while ascribing to the idea of a unified India, retained their unique ethnic groups and languages. Post-1947 history, which fulfills the national projects of Hindu India and Islamic Pakistan, fails to adequately acknowledge the shared cultural roots and traditions of the broader Punjabi community. This polarization of people attempts to homogenize the population and endanger the essence of the plurality which has existed in Punjab for centuries. During Partition, the migrants experienced intense trauma arising from loss of life, loss of property, and being forcibly removed from their ancestral homes. For both Hindu India and Islamic Pakistan, it was important to establish an independent national identity; re-imagining the past and creating a new national history allowed this new identity to emerge and reinforce and justify the nascent nation-state. Thus, the dominance and glorification of the "great men" such as Jinnah, Gandhi, and Nehru are palpable in the post-independence histories of India and Pakistan.

The promises made by the Indian elites were quickly and conveniently forgotten following Indian independence, as the Sikhs were dismissed by Nehru, who when reminded of his authoritative declaration that the Sikhs were entitled to the "glow of freedom" of India, claimed "that the circumstances had now changed" (Singh 1960, 30). Indeed, just how far these circumstances had changed could be seen from the very moment India became an independent nation. Almost immediately after the Partition (October 1947), Indian authorities, under the leadership of Prime Minister Jawaharlal Nehru, Home Minister Vallabhai Patel, and Punjab Governor Chandu Lal Trivedi, issued a directive circulated to all district magistrates in India designed to degrade and dehumanize the Sikh community. The issue read: "Sikhs as a community are a lawless people and are a menace to the law-abiding Hindus in the province. Deputy Commissioners should take special measures against them" (Singh 1989, 51). Those who did not comply with the directive were alienated and heavily fined. In 1948, Diwan Ram Lal, a Chief Justice of the Punjab High Court, once publicly claimed that "what a free India needs most urgently is barbers and more barbers to shingle and shave the Sikhs to apostatize them as Hindus" (Dhillon 1996, 42). The blatant disregard for democratic principles and freedoms within the formative stages of the "world's largest democracy," and the repeated attempts to catch the Sikh religion and culture in the net of the Hindu culture only heightened tensions between Hindus and Sikhs.

Sikhism Under the Indian Constitution

This failure to live up to these promises of recognition and autonomy is well-evidenced in the legal structures that the new

Indian Constitution eventually put in place. Unlike Kashmir, Punjab state was accorded no special "status" within the new federal structure, but rather treated worse than other Indian states. Moreover, as the first census conducted in Independent India revealed in 1951, the borders of this new state left Sikhs at a distinct political disadvantage. While 80 percent of all Sikhs resided in the Indian Punjab, they also comprised only about 35 percent of the newly-formed Punjab population, with Hindus accounting for 62 percent (Mahmood 1997, 114). In what can only be compared to gerrymandering, the Sikhs could not form a majority in any state and would only be able to elect representatives in only a few constituencies in Punjab where they were concentrated. Cynthia Keppley Mahmood describes this as "one of the great inadequacies of democratic representation based on demography" (1997, 113). Mahmood concludes that "the point drawn from this was that because of numbers the Sikhs might be left without effective representation" (1997, 114) and the Sikhs did indeed find themselves lacking appropriate representation in the national Parliament of India.

Not only was there no "special consideration" for a territory for the Sikhs, but—to add insult to injury—under Article 25(b) of the Constitution, which states that Sikhs, along with Jains and Buddhists are considered to be Hindus. The principle thus constitutionally established is that Sikhs are a subset of the Hindu religion, rather than a distinct entity. Moreover, as a consequence of this legal definition, Sikh life was now to be regulated by a variety of acts established specifically for Hindus, particularly in domestic and familial affairs, including:

- Hindu Marriage Act (relating to the marriage between Hindus)
- Hindu Minority and Guardianship Act
- Hindu Succession Act (relating to death without an established will)

- Hindu Adoption and Maintenance Act

The language of such acts is itself telling. Hindu and Sikh marriage rituals, for example, differ substantially. Whereas Hindus circumambulate in seven steps around a sacred fire, a Sikh bride and groom walk around the Guru Granth Sahib without a prescribed number of steps, thereby symbolizing not only their commitment to each other but their commitment to the Guru and Sikh community. Yet, in the Hindu Marriage Act, it is the Hindu practice of "saptapadi" (seven steps) which receives explicit mention (1955 Hindu Marriage Act, 7.2), while the acknowledgment of Sikh rituals can (at best) be found under provisions validating any long-established "custom and usage" within a "Hindu" community (1955 Hindu Marriage Act, 3. A). In this way, both the Indian Constitution and subsequent legislation attempt to cast the true principles and concepts of the Sikh religion in a different light, treating them as mere variations or derivatives of the Hindu mainstream, rather than a rejection of it. Thus, at the signing of the Indian Constitution, the Sikh community, through its two representatives, refused to sign, vehemently declaring that "the Sikhs do not accept this constitution" (Sikh Federation UK 2007, Annex A).

Interestingly, Sikhs are marked out to be subsumed under a broader "Hindu" identity, whereas Muslims, Christians, Parsis, and Jews were allowed to maintain their own sets of domestic and familial laws. It is this fact that informs the ire of Sikh historian and writer Ajmer Singh when he states that "as long as Hindus did not hold political power, their fascist thoughts were subdued. But as soon as they were granted political power in 1947, this fascist snakehead emerged, and the authoritarian will to assimilate other cultures took hold" (Singh 2009, 74).

Quite often the broadminded, multicultural, or "secular" ideals espoused by nationalist leaders such as Nehru and Gandhi are contrasted with the narrow-minded and chauvinist views of individuals such as Vinayak Damodar Savarkar (e.g.

Khilnani 2007). As the very structure of the Indian constitution suggests, however, this division might not be as clear-cut as it might initially seem. Indeed, even the most avowedly multicultural of India's Hindu leaders seem to have been vexed by the anxiety of ensuring that "Hindu" identity would be defined in such a way that its status as the "majority" religion within newly independent India would be safeguarded.

This very notion of the "Hindu majority" would play a crucial part in the rise of the Hindu nationalist Bharatiya Janata Party (BJP) in the late 1980s, as well as its spectacular resurgence in 2014, when the party succeeded in overturning supposed hegemony of "coalition politics" in India's Parliament and established a single-party government (Adeney & Sáez 2015). The electoral victories laid the groundwork for a resurgence of Hindu nationalism and its quest for political hegemony, with right-wing nationalists believing that Hindu identity has the potential to foster a coherent national community that will produce stability and prosperity. Since the BJP's 2014 and 2019 victories under Narendra Modi, the party has acted swiftly and surely to implement certain Hindu nationalist policies. Particularly prominent among such policies is the repeal of Article 370, which granted a special status to the contested area of Jammu and Kashmir by conferring upon it the power to retain a separate constitution, state flag, and autonomy over internal matters. This action undermined India's original promise of asymmetric federalism to the region while leaving other asymmetric arrangements untouched, creating the perception that the repeal was justified because Jammu and Kashmir was India's only Muslim-majority state. Such moves have further hurt India's already crippled democracy, pushing it further from the model of a state-nation and towards a nation-state. The lack of representation for the Sikh community and its independence from Hinduism in the Indian Constitution is a testament to the long history of discrimination and marginalization of Sikhs.

Advocates of Hindu nationalism have long resisted the state-nation model, attempting to replicate European-style nationalism based on religious identity, language, and racial unity. This borderline ethnonationalism in India ultimately attempts to engulf all religions under the umbrella "Hindu" religion, as has been done with the Buddhist religion, or to annihilate those who fail to assimilate, as has been attempted with the Sikhs. Indian politician Vinayak Damodar Savarkar's motto of "Hindu, Hindi, Hindustan" provides fuel to Hindu nationalists to whom patriotism and loyalty to a "unified Hindu nation" is of utmost importance. This, along with Mahatma Gandhi's ignorant claims that the Sikh Gurus were Hindus and that Sikhism was a part of a broader Hindu tradition (Gandhi 1989, 263), lent credence to the Hindu nationalist movement that rose to political prominence upon the back of ethnic, religious, caste polarization in the 1980s and advocated for the prioritization of Indian nationalism over communal impulses. Leaders of the majority community view cultural pluralism as a threat to the unity of the nation, combating it with nationalism as a method to cope with the internal divisions of their own community and to avoid questions about the policies of the state, often resorting to extreme violence to protect the "security of the State." While the Hindu community undoubtedly suffers internal conflicts (from upper and lower caste clashes, language, aristocratic values, etc.), its common understanding and united front in opposition to minority groups such as the Sikhs are notable. English writer Samuel Johnson famously declared that "patriotism is the last refuge of a scoundrel" (Boswell 1923, 224). Particularly in India, patriotism and nationalism are often used to brush aside inconvenient facts of state-sponsored violence and terrorism.

Mahmood also argues that, in light of the broader trends and institutional discrimination against the Sikhs, it quickly becomes apparent that the Indian secular state and the tolerant Hindu community are not what they seem at first glance. "It is becoming clearer to many observers, for example, that the philosophical tolerance of the Hindu tradition, emphasized by many Western admirers, is not in fact matched by a social or political tolerance for non-Hindu groups," but rather a version of "ethnic exclusivism" (Mahmood 1997, 118). In his work *Utopias in Conflict* (2018), Ainslie Embree recognizes that this aspect of the Hindu culture has played a central role in modern communal conflicts throughout the subcontinent. In Mahmood's assessment, "he notes that the philosophical willingness to accept many kinds of truths as meaningful is the source of the 'mistaken' notion of Hindu tolerance, which assumes a live-and-let-live generosity" (Mahmood 1997, 118). In fact, a more genuine view of the purported Hindu tolerance would be that different truths and social practices are "encapsulated" within a broader Hindu umbrella—as is the case with Buddhists and Jains. There are even Hindus who talk of "Hindu Muslims," which, for Muslims, who do not accept the very premise of the overarching Hindu framework, is not only ridiculous but insulting and sacrilegious. This spiritual imperialism has dominated all aspects of the Indian government and is most prominent within the justice system. As Mahmood concludes, "to ignore the religion/political axis in the majority community wrongly places the burden to defend or explain this nexus on the activist minority alone. When we ask why the Sikhs express religious and political grievances in joint terms, we have to ask how it is that religious and political dominance are intertwined in the Indian state" (Mahmood 1997, 120).

Before passing on to the consequences that resulted from these failed attempts at Hindu assimilation, it bears mentioning that Sikh discontent with their position under the new Indian state has by no means dampened their willingness to sacrifice for the new Indian nation. To give a critical example, Sikhs have remained an outsized presence in India's armed forces, ready and willing to bring their martial ethos to bear for the democratic state. Even here, however, it is clear that discrimination was rooted in the cultural grain of the state. In *Fighting for Faith and Nation,* Mahmood recounts the testimony of a retired Indian army colonel, who referred to the performance of the Sikh soldiers in the 1965 war as "dazzling," but also noted the disillusionment of Sikhs in the Indian army: "'They feel,' he asserted, 'that their service through multiple wars since independence is at this point not only not being rewarded but is being mocked because of suspicion of their [separatist] sympathies. This suspicion... which results in being passed over for promotions and otherwise side-stepped in the military scheme of things, is much more a source of alienation than the actual [separatist] movement ever would have been.' A second retired officer... entirely agreed with this assessment" (Mahmood 1997, 115). The failed project of Hindu assimilation, in other words, would become the grounds of anti-Sikh discrimination, discrimination which not only alienated the Sikhs from the Indian mainstream but also pushed them to increasingly advocate for legal and political reforms that would ensure their identity and autonomy.

During the creation of the Indian state, Sikhs and other minorities were presented as a threat to unity. Within a year after Indian independence, Sikhs were declared to be a "criminal tribe" by Prime Minister Jawaharlal Nehru. The Indian government also implemented several new laws in order to criminalize citizens arbitrarily—unsurprisingly, these laws tended to disproportionately affect the Sikh community, which constituted a sizable portion of the protests against Indira Gandhi's Emergency. The degradation of democracy and due process under the guise of national security and citizen safety was instrumental in Indira Gandhi's implementation of the President's Rule over India and Punjab. Additionally, the situation in the freshly partitioned India was exacerbated by the

Bharatiya Jana Sangh (the predecessor of the Bharatiya Janata Party of the present day), which attempted to claim the entirety of Indian heritage as Hindu heritage and the Indian state as a Hindu state, giving rise to the modern right-wing Hindu extremism. The Bharatiya Jana Sangh was linked to the Hindu militant organization Rashtriya Swayamsevak Sangh (RSS), one of whose members killed Mahatma Gandhi for being too conciliatory to Muslims; the organization spearheaded the campaign for Hindu domination throughout all of India, particularly in Punjab, where the majority of Sikhs resided.

CHAPTER 4

Sikhism under the Indian Nation-State

Chapter 4

Sikhism under the Indian Nation-State

Following the framing of the Indian Constitution in 1947, it became clear that the Indian national leaders had little interest in recognizing Sikh demands for autonomy in the Punjab region, as originally promised during the nationalist movement. In fact, quite the opposite occurred. Through what can only be described as a duplicitous sleight-of-hand, these very same demands were reframed as evidence of Sikhs' supposedly "secessionist" and "anti-national" tendencies. The Indian government's reaction to the Anandpur Sahib Resolution of 1973 is extremely revealing in this regard. Written against the backdrop of increasing activity by Christian and Hindu missionaries in the Sikh community, as well as the aftereffects of Partition on the Sikhs, the document sought to secure the place of a community still struggling to find its role in the new nation-state of India. The Resolution did so by proposing reforms and policy goals aimed at further increasing the autonomy of the Punjab region as well as eliminating poverty and starvation, increasing healthcare capabilities, and eradicating the caste system. This increasing pressure for internal self-determination was pursued through decades of peaceful protests and negotiation with the central government, but these demands were never seriously considered or addressed. Instead, the central government increasingly framed such demands as evidence of separatist tendencies that justified harsh repressive measures.

When evaluating these political tensions, it is important to consider the geographic location and significance of the majority-Sikh region of Punjab. Although Punjab covers only 1.5% of India's land, it is one of the most fertile areas in the Indian subcontinent, producing nearly 20% of the nation's wheat and 12% of its rice. Contributing nearly $80 billion to the national GDP, the Punjab region is considered the "breadbasket of India," and is undoubtedly critical to the Indian economy. As a result, Joyce Pettigrew reports, "the area experienced a high degree of centralized control over its resources, water, power, and agricultural produce" (Pettigrew 1995, 4-5), imposing a political hindrance on Punjab's economic and social development. The central government regulated the amount of water Punjab could take from its own rivers, and it was calculated that "75% of available waters of riparian Punjab were allotted to non-riparian states" (Pettigrew 1995, 4-5). On top of this, central government investment in Punjab, which was 2% in 1980, fell to just .8% over the next ten years as the central government returned to Punjab an investment of only one-third of what the state had contributed. These centralization policies were the perfect formula for generating discontent throughout the Sikh community, and in 1982, Sikh leaders commenced mass protests pushing for historic rights. The Indian government responded by criminalizing and demonizing the peaceful agitation, arresting over 300,000 people, and instigating violence through proxy agencies in attempts to discredit the movement.

The 1970s and early 1980s can thus be pinpointed as the period in which incipient tensions between Sikhs and the Hindu-dominated state escalated, largely due to the inflammatory comments from government leaders. American anthropologist Clifford Geertz notes that identification with "the nation" —as represented by cultural tradition, religion, history, and language—remains difficult for minority group[s] if elites have strong ties with the hegemonic culture. This accurately represents the Sikh position at the beginning of the 1970s. In the course of the next ten years, the elite's mental and emotional ties to the state perceptibly began to weaken, though they made no commitment to push for extreme change that did not fall within the limits of the Constitution.

An important turning point in this relationship would come in the "Emergency" period of 1975-1977. In 1975, when a high court barred Indira Gandhi from holding office due to election inconsistencies, she responded by using her power as Prime Minister to declare a national State of Emergency, assuming absolute control over the country. Civil liberties were suspended, political opponents were arrested, and journalists were jailed. The Maintenance of Internal Security Act (MISA), which had been established in 1969, was strengthened in 1975 when Indira Gandhi declared a national emergency. MISA was aggressively used against political opponents, trade unions, and civil society groups that challenged the government. While it was later repealed, the damage of the legislation had already dealt a crippling blow to the democratic rights of the people.

These actions emboldened right-wing Hindus both outside of, and within, Indira Gandhi's Indian National Congress Party. For example, Swami Adityavesh, a right-wing Hindu politician of the Congress party, demanded that Sikhs be expelled from Haryana to Punjab (Sandhu 1999, 332). Kewal Krishan, another member of the Congress party in Punjab, threatened to destroy all Sikh organizations (ibid). Harbans Lal Khanna, a parliament member of the Bharatiya Janata Party in Punjab, stated publicly in Amritsar on 30 May 1981, *"Dukki tikki khehan nahin deni, sir te pagri rehan nahin deni; kachh, kara, kirpan; ehnoon bhejo Pakistan!"* (We will not let any second or third group exist, we will not leave a turban on any head; the Kacchera, the Kara, the Kirpan, [5 Ks] send these to Pakistan) (Dhillon 1996, 375). He also encouraged the desecration of a model of the Golden Temple by a mob.

Particularly in the early 1980s, Sikhs were accused of terrorist attacks or instigating violence during peaceful protests, claims that became very pronounced in 1983. A post-1984 SGPC White

Paper reported that discarded turbans, pistols, and cartridges were found at certain crime scenes (Dhillon 1996), and the Akali Dal Party alleged that the attacks and violence were perpetrated not by Sikhs, but by professionals of the Third Agency (an intelligence wing formed by Indira Gandhi during the Emergency), to create a pretext to impose the President's rule in Punjab, which she eventually did on October 6th, 1983. However, with a lack of due process and the government's failure to launch further investigations into these events, it was impossible to garner significant public attention outside of the Sikh community. With false-flag operations executed by the Indian government, communal trust between Hindus and Sikhs in Punjab rapidly deteriorated, isolating the Sikh community and marking them as untrustworthy. The government's narrative aimed to demonize and vilify the Sikh community, ensuring Indira Gandhi's freedom to assert authoritarian control and justify military attacks on the most revered institutions of the faith, which she would do in 1984.

Ironically, it was only *after* 1984 that the Sikh masses took to new political alignments, with the elite participating from the sidelines only when it was safe to do so. In this regard, the Indian state produced exactly the kind of radicalism it claimed to be attacking, as ordinary Sikhs lost faith in the potential for reform, and instead began to call for revolution. Right-wing Hindu organizations seized upon this opportunity to further propagate their agenda of "Hindi, Hindu, Hindustan," encouraging the othering of those communities which refused to consider themselves as Hindu or who speak mother tongues other than Hindi. Inevitably, tensions increased between Hindu and Sikh populations, even those who were uninvolved or uninterested in conflict. In this context, the stage had been set. The Sikh community had been dehumanized, their protests de-legitimized, and polarization between the minority and majority reached nearly unprecedented levels as the Sikhs resisted attempts at repression and assimilation by the Hindu-led state.

In the next chapter, we will bear witness to the grisly events in which these dynamics of repression, alienation, and vilification culminated in 1984. Here, however, we focus on examining the genesis of tensions between the Sikhs and Indian state in the 1970s and the increasingly large rift they produced in the 1980s. More specifically, we aim to show how the Indian state escalated these conflicts and tensions over a legitimate set of demands from the Sikh community, demands that emerged from the result of the broken promises of the Indian nationalist movement examined in the previous chapter.

The Anandpur Resolution

Perhaps the clearest articulation of Sikh demands *vis-a-vis* the Indian state was the Anandpur Resolution of 1973, aptly named after the city in which the Tenth Guru founded the Khalsa. Broadly speaking, the Anandpur Resolution was a list of goals made by the Akali Dal; the self-appointed political party of the Sikhs. Notably, the resolution declared its goals within the context of reforming state, federal, and constitutional structures, and did not include any mention of Sikh independence. Nevertheless, Indira Gandhi and the Indian National Congress party denounced it as a secessionist document. Simultaneously, what initially began as a political document aimed at outlining and directing the goals of the Akali Dal party specifically, rapidly became a lodestone for the Sikh community as a whole.

In this manner, the Anandpur Resolution came to serve as a list of long-term goals for the Punjab region, and the role of the Indian state in the future of Punjab. Addressing India's treatment of the lower castes, discrimination faced by Indian ethnic and religious minorities, and the capitalist monopolies entrenched within the economy, the document faced significant backlash from the Hindu ruling parties. In addition, the

Resolution also demanded an end to the redirection of Punjab's rivers to other states at the expense of Punjab's citizens. Through this push for greater state autonomy and decreased central government rule, the document aimed to release majority-Sikh Punjab from the overweening control of the Hindu state and fulfill the promises made to Sikhs by the nationalist movement.

One of the key figures in bringing awareness to the Anandpur Resolution was a young Jarnail Singh Bhindranwale, the charismatic religious leader of the prominent orthodox Sikh institution known as the Damdami Taksal. Known for his fiery speeches and successes in persuading Punjab's youth to abandon drugs, alcohol, and consumerism, Bhindranwale's commitment to the Sikh community and faith was well recognized, and his support for the Anandpur resolution played a critical role in its popularization. Touring villages throughout Punjab, his meetings were attended by throngs of faithful Sikhs and curious audiences. He advocated against rising substance abuse, alcohol, and pornography, instead encouraging Sikhs to get baptized and adopt the turban and beard. In a time when many leaders were not engaged directly with the community, Bhindranwale embodied the qualities of a true leader and Sikh, traveling relentlessly from city to city instead of delegating and making empty promises from the comfort of office or gurdwara.

Showing no interest in a political career, Bhindranwale instead immersed himself in preaching and community organizing. The fact that he retained his popularity and fame despite constant smear campaigns and propaganda from the Indian government speaks strongly to the Sikhs' rising frustration with the state and its discrimination against the community.

Over time, the Sikh community's respect and admiration for Bhindranwale irked *both* the Akali Dal *and* the Congress Party, as his views on the Indian state's injustices and his unwillingness to play the political game threatened the norm.

Part of this irritation owed to the class dimension of Bhindranwale's supporters:

> *The backbone of [Bhindranwale] are the sons and daughters of Punjab's middle and low-level peasantry and agricultural workers. The challenge to the Akali and SGPC [an institution in charge of the management of Gurdwaras in Punjab, Haryana, Chandigarh, and Himachal Pradesh, implemented by the British] leadership... comes from what was once its base - the small and middle peasants. The socio-economic roots of [Bhindranwale] are totally different from [the Akali leaders] ... all of whom come from the landed gentry classes of the state. (Telford 1992, 983)*

Described as having "unflinching zeal and firm convictions," Bhindranwale did "not succumb to the pressure of big-wigs in the Akali Party nor could he be manipulated by the authorities to serve their ends" (Dhillon 1996). According to Gurdarshan Singh,

> *Those who tried to mend him or bend him to suit their designs underestimated his tremendous will and ultimately lost their own ground. He never became their tool. People who promoted his cause or helped him to rise to prominence were disillusioned, when he refused to play second fiddle to them and declined to tread the path laid down for him. Paradoxical though it may seem, they became his unwilling tools. Thousands listened to him with rapt attention at [his sermons]. He had tremendous power to mobilize the masses. His charisma and eloquence overshadowed other leaders. (ibid)*

A staunch advocate of the Anandpur Resolution, Bhindranwale launched the Dharam Yudh Morcha, a political movement that galvanized the youth of Punjab, leading to mass protests with thousands on the streets. As we have seen, Sikhism's structure and culture are inherently political, making Bhindranwale's call to action resonate even with politically apathetic Sikhs. While the Resolution addressed several issues within the state, the most important topics were those of irrigation rights and discrimination against religious minorities and lower castes. However, Indira Gandhi labeled the Resolution—and those who supported it—as secessionist, and government politicians quickly fell in line as a result (Shani 2008, 51-60). As the Sikh public support for the Resolution became clear, Bhindranwale took the mantle, becoming its primary advocate, and thus a prime target for the Indian government's propaganda. The demonization of the supporters of the document and vague judicial laws, coupled with Indira Gandhi's self-proclaimed State of Emergency, led to rising tensions between the Sikhs and the Indian government. By early October of 1982, more than 25,000 Akali workers courted arrest in Punjab in support of the agitation. Out of 220 deaths during the first 19 months of the Dharam Yudh Morcha, 190 had been Sikhs (Dhillon 1996).

The Vilification of Jarnail Singh

The Punjab police, due to colonial practices carried over from the turbulent years of British rule, and encouraged by politicians and the new Indian judicial system, had disconcertingly free reign to act than in other provinces (Dhillon 2006). Rounding up and illegally detaining suspects for prolonged aggressive interrogations, as well as killing (rather than arresting) suspects in pre-planned "staged encounters" were common practices for the Punjab police, and still continue to this day. Such practices led to an erosion of trust between law enforcement and citizens, with Sikhs, in particular, having little faith in filing complaints or information requests with the police, due to the blatantly lawless activity being sanctioned by the state police leadership. With the increased protests from the Sikh community and Indira's State of Emergency, police violence and harassment increased, particularly toward the Sikhs who wore the 5 K's, who formed a core part of Bhindranwale's base. Under the guise of maintaining law and order, the actions of the state police escalated in the form of false encounters, tortures, and killings in police custody, as well as extrajudicial police invasions and oppressive lockdowns in rural Punjab (Dhillon 1996). This too, was a part of the government's campaign to delegitimize and dehumanize the Sikh community in the eyes of the public, further elevating Hindu-Sikh tensions in the general population. Bhindranwale openly spoke of police-staged crimes, in which Sikhs were accused of theft or violence with the intention of linking the falsely accused to Bhindranwale, as well as the fact that many of the Sikhs arrested on false accusations were tortured and killed.

Part of the reason police were able to operate with such impunity was the wide latitude given to them, and other state agencies, by a set of draconian national security laws. One of the most critical was the 1967 Unlawful Activities Prevention Act (UAPA), which replaced previous preventive detention laws and was cited in several cases registered against Sikh political prisoners. The Act gave the State the authority to declare organizations unlawful for a broad spectrum of reasons, and then limit and scrutinize their members. Under UAPA, bail is notoriously difficult to obtain, and those who are accused can be held in custody for six months without even filing charges. As a preventive detention law, UAPA has been repeatedly misused and has led to politically-motivated detentions and human rights violations. Moreover, by removing the periodic review clause typical of such detention legislation, the UAPA remains valid indefinitely, unless directly repealed in Parliament. Alongside the UAPA, the 1958 Armed Forces Special Powers Act (AFSPA)—created specifically to address separatist movements—empowered the military with a greater power to use force against civilians than the police. Between 1983 to 1987, an iteration of AFSPA was in full force in Punjab, and in 1990, the Act was introduced in Jammu and Kashmir.

These older pieces of legislation were supplemented by new laws introduced in the 1980s. The National Security Act (NSA) instituted in 1980 granted the State preventive detention power even more extensive than UAPA and similarly removed any requirement for periodic Parliamentary review. The NSA gave power to the central and state governments to detain individuals for a maximum period of 12 months, during which information supporting the detention could be withheld in "public interest" and a detained person could be denied a lawyer. On top of this, the Terrorist and Disruptive Activities Prevention Act (TADA) was instituted in the mid-1980s when Sikh protests began to peak. "Disruptive Activities" was deliberately defined vaguely to include a wide variety of actions, including any form of protest. Under the law, special TADA courts were set up to prosecute those accused of terrorist activities in areas designated by the national government as "terrorist affected areas," often disproportionately targetting minority communities (Sivapalan & Sabhaney 2019).

According to one source, "TADA created new criminal offenses, enhanced procedural powers for the police, and reduced protections for defendants. Under TADA, confessions made before police officers were admissible as evidence, which facilitated custodial abuse and torture" (ibid). Under the guise of fighting terrorism, authorities unjustly detained young men from marginalized communities. "Over 76,000 people were arrested while TADA was in force from 1985 to 1995. The conviction rate for these arrests was less than one percent, which meant thousands were wrongfully incarcerated" (ibid). Most significantly, the expedited system set up for TADA completely swamped the normal judicial channels. "Suddenly, there was no more crime in Punjab, only terrorism," said a former police officer (Mahmood 1997, 98).

Although the authoritarian powers these laws granted to the

state is itself concerning, the disparity in their use and enforcement is even more disturbing. Speaking on the double standards of the Indian government's handling of cases that involved Hindus and Sikhs, ex-Provincial Service Officer A.R. Darshi reports that Bhindranwale referred to the following examples of discrimination:

> [In the case of] Ashok Kumar, a criminal and Brahmin by caste, who was shot dead by police in 1983 after attempting to commit arson, the Union Home Minister quickly rushed to the city of Patiala to conduct an investigation; on the other hand, when nearly two hundred Sikhs were killed by police during the Dharam Yudh Morcha, there was no formal inquiry and no acknowledgment from the central government.
>
> Pawan Kumar Sharma, another Brahmin from Patiala, was discovered having smuggled 230 high explosive hand grenades. He was freed without a single case being registered against him. On the other hand, a Sikh soldier, Piara Singh of Ferozpur, was accused of stealing a sten gun; the gun was later recovered from the residence of a Hindu soldier, but Piara Singh was tortured to death by a Hindu officer.
>
> [During Jarnail Singh's residency in the Akal Takht complex] Union Home Minister P.C. Sethi threatened to have Jarnail Singh forcibly dragged out of the Akal Takht complex within a week. In response, Bhindranwale, challenging Sethi to come try to remove him, instantly had a criminal case registered against him while no action was taken against Sethi. (Darshi 2004, 54-55)

Clearly, the framework of India's "security" legislation is not restricted to simply one or two laws but is instead a persistent and unstoppable force frequently used against minority communities and dissidents critical of the Indian government. The targeted, systemic discrimination of the Sikhs, cloaked as a moral necessity in the prevention of terrorism and threats to the security of the State, has destroyed entire villages and crippled families for generations to come.

Against this backdrop, it should come as little surprise that Bhindranwale spoke strongly against police attacks not just on individuals, but on the Sikh religion and community as a whole. These attacks included the burning of buses containing Sikh scriptures, and Sikh train passengers being singled out and beaten under false pretenses. It was clear that the Sikh identity was under attack and that the government's attempt at alienating the community was working. A team sponsored by the People's Union for Civil Liberties, an organization founded in 1976 with former Indian Justice V. M. Tarkunde as Chairman, reported the police excesses against Sikhs prior to and after 1984:

> We had no hesitation in saying in our report that the police had behaved like a barbarian force out for revenge. They had even set houses of a few absconders on fire and destroyed utensils, clothes, and whatever else they found in them. Relatives of the absconders were harassed and even detained. Even many days after the excesses committed by the police, we could see how fear-stricken the people were. Villagers gave us the names of some of the police sub-inspectors and deputy superintendents involved; some of them, they said, had a reputation of taking the law into their hands. (Dhillon 1996)

The Sikhs' aggravation was only increased during the 1982 Asian Games, in which all Sikhs, regardless of social position, whether retired military, politician, or ordinary citizens, were subjected to invasive frisking and the removal of their turbans (Grewal 1998, 205-241). Sikhs traveling from Punjab to Delhi, or back, were indiscriminately stopped, searched, and humiliated, and Sikhs understood this humiliation not just individually but as a community. According to journalist Kuldip Nayyar, "from that day their feeling of alienation [had] been increasing" (Grewal 1998, 223). It is unsurprising that Bhindranwale's support continued to increase given his dedication to upholding Sikh values and identity, which were to be protected, even if by force. While other Sikh leaders cowed to the demands of Indira

Gandhi, Bhindranwale remained steadfast in his convictions and support for the Anandpur Resolution, serving as inspiration for a community increasingly discontent with its treatment. According to Kirpal Dhillon, a report in 1984 from two respected journalists denounced the government's tendency to quickly attribute the slightest increases in even normal crime to the Sikhs, writing, "objection is taken in Punjab to the tendency to ascribe all crime to Sikh extremists. The press must be wary of such stereotypes. Many crimes, robberies, and murders have little to do with the current political scene" (Dhillon 2006, 129).

It was the threat that Bhindranwale posed to the Indian elite that led to his subsequent vilification, making him a primary source against whom all accusations of Sikh violence were directed. Despite having no involvement in the violence against Hindus, and, in fact, denouncing the criminal acts of those who killed innocents, politicians throughout India, particularly Indira Gandhi, continued to label him a terrorist and secessionist. On numerous occasions, Bhindranwale would state, "It suits the government to publicize me as an extremist, thus making an excuse to frustrate the just cause and the legitimate demands of the entire Sikh community and Punjab state" (Sathananthan et al. 1983) The attacks on Jarnail Singh Bhindranwale, the key leader of the Sikhs, aimed to delegitimize the movement for the autonomy and rights of the Sikh people, portraying him as a religious fanatic eager to destroy the fabric of the Indian nation-state. Bhindranwale's position on the Hindu-Sikh relations and Indira Gandhi's role in the inflammation of tensions can be summarized in his 1982 statement for *India Today*:

> We [the Sikhs advocating for the Anandpur Resolution] are no extremists or communalists. Give us one instance when we insulted or hit anyone. But the Government terms us extremists. We are extremists if we protest when our Gurus are painted as lovers of wine and women by the Lala's [Lala Jagat Narain was editor of a popular right-wing Hindu newspaper

that slandered the Sikh Gurus and called for the discrimination against Sikhs] newspapers. I preach that all Sikhs must observe their tenets and be the Guru's warriors. Let all Hindus wear their sacred thread and put tilak on their foreheads, we shall honor them. I stand for Hindu-Sikh unity. Let the Hindus at least once declare that they stand for Sikh-Hindu unity. Let the prime minister, whose forefathers our Guru Tegh Bahadur saved by sacrificing his life [reference to the ninth Guru's sacrifice for the freedom of the Hindu faith], declare that she is for unity. (Thukral 1982)

In February of 1983, Bhindranwale gave a galvanizing speech openly calling Sikhs in Punjab "slaves," outlining the discriminatory judicial system, criminal police force, Indira Gandhi's rebuke of the Anandpur Sahib Resolution's demands, and economic measures taken by the government to suppress Punjabi prosperity, as well as past struggles in post-Independence India by Sikhs to ensure their most basic rights, including the protests against political and economic suppression since the 1960s: "How shall we get rid of this curse of slavery? If you wish to speak Punjabi, if you want a Punjabi-speaking state demarcated… eighty-six thousand of you [have been sent] to jail, over one hundred and thirteen shed your blood and achieved martyrdom and still there is no announcement from Indira" (Sandhu 1999, 46). It is unsurprising that, by this point, many Sikhs considered themselves as being treated as they were second-class citizens in a country they had disproportionately contributed to the freedom of.

Aside from direct state action, the Indian government's unequal response to the deaths of Hindus and Sikhs is striking; the administration's blatant disregard for Sikh lives frustrated the community and further contributed to the feeling of being second-class citizens. In one incident in 1983, seven Hindu citizens were shot in a bus; the attacks, blamed on Bhindranwale, were immediately officially condemned by himself and nearly every other Sikh group. However, as Bhindranwale revealed, the Indian government's immediate response to the event left troubling questions about the loyalties of the nation's leaders. *Someone killed seven Hindus on a bus. No Sikh has said this was good, everyone deplored it. But because seven Hindus had died, not twenty-four hours passed [before swift government action]. The Ministry was dissolved. [Indira Gandhi's] rule was imposed. The [Punjab] region was declared disturbed. However, one hundred and fifty Sikhs died and not even one man was charged. Now all of you Sikhs should sit down and figure out as to what the thoughts of this Government of the Hindus are about the turban and the beard [markers of Sikhs]. (Sandhu 1999, 308)*

Bhindranwale, who had since 1982 resided in the Golden Temple complex (among the many buildings historically used to provide shelter to pilgrims) with about 200 other Sikhs, perfectly positioned himself to reach the masses of the community while making bold political and religious statements. Holding his sermons at the Akal Takht, Bhindranwale's nod to the historical significance of the institution as the political and military authority of the Sikhs amplified his message to the community while making him a bigger target still for the Indian government. A common justification for the 1984 attack on the Golden Temple complex refers to Bhindranwale's armed occupation of a religious temple; it should, however, be noted that he resided not in the Harmandir Sahib, but on the upper floors of the Akal Takht at the invitation of the President of the committee charged with the operations of the complex. The weapons and arming of Sikhs within the Akal Takht complex, moreover, held historical precedent: the sixth Guru himself housed and trained his army in the complex, and the Gurus in fact encouraged and required the militarization of the Sikhs in order to promote self-defense. The justifications of those attempting to condone the events of

1984 often lack an understanding of the Sikh culture or the need for protection in a hostile political climate as state-sanctioned propaganda and extra-judicial killings threatened the very existence of the community.

It is also important to note that while reports of insurgency and extremist militarism are often cited by the Indian government and its supporters with the intention of denouncing Bhindranwale and the Sikhs of the Dharam Yudh Morcha, these reports are often inaccurate and misrepresentative of the Sikh culture. While calls for an independent Sikh nation did increase in some quarters through the 1970s and 80s, they remained a minority position. Moreover, even such advocates justified these demands in terms of the broken promises of the Indian government and the foolish faith of Sikh leaders at the time of Partition. The harassment and demonization of the Sikhs elevated these ideas of freedom and gave them credibility. However, the vast majority of Sikhs, including Bhindranwale himself, never demanded the creation of a separate nation-state. In fact, when asked about his views on Khalistan, an independent Sikh homeland, Bhindranwale stated:

Brothers, I don't oppose it nor do I support it. We are silent. However, one thing is definite, if this time the Queen of India does give [Khalistan] to us, we shall certainly take it. We won't reject it. We shall not repeat the mistake of 1947 [in which Sikh leadership elected to remain with India]. As yet, we do not ask for it. It is Indira Gandhi's business and not mine, nor Longowal's [Akali Dal leader], nor of any other of our leaders. It is Indira's business, Indira should tell us whether she wants to keep us in Hindustan or not. We like to live together [with the rest of the Indians]; we like to live in India. (Dhillon 1996, 186)

Prophesying what would become a full-blown independence movement following the attacks on the Golden Temple, Bhindranwale said "if the Indian Government invades the [Harmandir Sahib] complex, the foundation for an independent

Sikh state will have been laid" (Sandhu 1999, lvii) As the Indian government proceeded to attack the Golden Temple on June 1st, Akal Takht, and dozens of other Gurdwaras throughout Punjab, irreparably damaging the relationship between the Sikhs and the Indian government, calls for independence skyrocketed. After all, how could the Sikh community peaceably live in India when their own nation's military had just stormed, murdered, and taken control of the most significant religious institutions of the culture?

While blaming Bhindranwale for Hindu-Sikh tensions, political turbulence, and subsequent attacks on Sikh Gurdwaras is exceedingly common, evidence suggests that the Indian government was, in fact, preparing for the attacks even prior to Bhindranwale's relocation to the Akal Takht complex. A New York Times article written just a few weeks prior to the military operation reported:

Before the raid on the Golden Temple, neither the Government nor anyone else appeared to put much credence in the Khalistan movement... Bhindranwale himself said many times that he was not seeking an independent country for Sikhs, merely greater autonomy for Punjab within the Indian Union... One possible explanation advanced for the Government's raising of the Khalistan question is that it needs to take every opportunity to justify the killing in Amritsar and the invasion of the Sikhs' holiest shrine. (Stevens 1984)

The Indian government created detailed and elaborate plans for an extensive military operation while calling for peace and feigning willingness to negotiate, denying any accusations and assuring the Sikhs that they had no intention of sending armed troops into the Golden Temple Complex. However, by the end of May 1984 six additional divisions of the army, including highly-specialized paramilitary commandos, were stationed in Punjab (Singh 1997, 352-354). In hindsight, it is incredibly obvious that the Indian government had no plans to truly

deescalate political tensions in Punjab in the months leading up
to the attack; Bhindranwale realized this too, as he began making
preparations for his final battle. In his final interview,
Bhindranwale predicted that the government was set on
genocide, stating, "[the Government doesn't] like the Sikhs and
they want to finish them off" (The MacNeil/Lehrer NewsHour,
1984). Punjab's borders were sealed off and intrastate movement
was disabled by the military, with the water and electricity to
the Golden Temple cut off.

Exploratory fire was attempted on June 4th, with initial army
commandos and tear gas proving ineffective on June 5th. The
use of tanks and heavy artillery on the complex began on June
6th, with tanks, and helicopters used to deter the thousands of
upset villagers who had attempted to gather in Amritsar. In
addition, such measures were taken at over three dozen other
Gurdwaras which had been preemptively attacked by the
government, which cited insurgents in each of the temples
(Grewal 1998 205-241). It is difficult to fathom how permanently
and deeply the actions of the Indian government affected the
Sikh psyche. Regardless of Jarnail Singh Bhindranwale's
presence in the Akal Takht complex, Indira Gandhi sought not
to deter the advocates of the Anandpur Resolution but to
completely and absolutely demolish the heart, spirit, identity,
and faith of the Sikh culture along with its institutions.

CHAPTER 5

Genocide III - 1984

Chapter 5

Genocide III - 1984

I n Punjab, where Sikhs hold a slim majority, the people have grown accustomed to annual monsoon rains marking the end of extreme heat in early June. But on the first of the month in 1984, they were greeted by a torrent of bullets and bombs from the artillery of their own nation. This full-scale army attack, codenamed "Operation Blue Star" by the Indian government, marked the beginning of years of gruesome organized violence against the Sikhs, and one of the most scarring events in the community's history. This would begin with the army's assault on the Golden Temple under Operation Blue Star, as well as its months-long mop-up operation across Punjab, Operation Woodrose. On October 31st, 1984, Prime Minister Indira Gandhi, at whose behest these operations had been carried out, was assassinated by her Sikh bodyguards. In the days that followed, anti-Sikh pogroms exploded across north India "as murders and atrocities occurred primarily in Delhi, but a similar pattern of violence prevailed in the Hindi-speaking heartland states of Bihar, Madhya Pradesh, Uttar Pradesh, and Haryana," leaving nearly 30,000 (according to unofficial figures) dead in the space of a mere four days (Van Dyke 1996, 201). Although this event would mark the end of the most visible and gratuitous violence, repressive action and killings by the Indian police and military would continue for years to come.

How are we to understand such violence? Since the colonial period, both popular and official perceptions of communal violence in India are often understood to be the work of impassioned crowds, "a faceless, aggressive, unfathomable, irrational compact of people" whose murderous actions against particular ethnic, caste, linguistic, or religious community are often justified based on the idea that the victims are collectively responsible for some kind of offense (e.g. an insult, a crime, a murder) committed by a member of their community (Hansen 2008, 2). As Paul Brass notes, however, this notion of the impassioned crowd essentially dissolves responsibility: "The struggle to control the representation of riots is also one to cast and divert blame. If the people are responsible, the government is not to blame... If the police are to blame, then the politicians are saved" (Brass 1996, 5). In reality, Brass argues, most riots in India are well-orchestrated and organized events, involving the systematic mobilization of rioters and demobilization of the police (usually by politicians), as well as precise targeting of victims rather than spontaneous and random violence (Brass 2003).

As we shall see in this chapter, the clear culpability of the Indian government and Indian National Congress party in instigating the events of 1984, as well as the brutal repression that followed, suggests that the real question is not if socially-organized "riots" or state-orchestrated "pogroms" occurred. Rather, the real question is whether all of these numerous, extensive, and well-planned campaigns of violence, taken together, constituted genocide—a systematic attempt to erase a given people from the face of the earth.

Under the framework of Dr. Gregory H. Stanton, President of the Genocide Watch, genocides (and attempted genocides) can be said to occur in eight "stages:" classification, symbolization, dehumanization, organization, polarization, preparation, extermination, and denial. In the first three stages, a given group of people is not only marked out as distinct from other populations but also maligned and disparaged as a whole; producing a notion of collective guilt that lays down the putative "justification" for their elimination. In the next two stages, the overarching framework for action against the community is established as the state not only lays the groundwork for a conflict but also polarizes other segments of the population against the target community. When these conflicts come to a head, detailed preparations are made and the execution of a campaign of extermination occurs—a process that may be more or less successful in its aims.

In the preceding chapters, we have already witnessed many of these stages were already well-established by 1984. Indeed, as far as classification and symbolization are concerned, the Hindu-dominated Indian state hardly needed to do any work, for from the very inception of their faith the Sikhs were already visibly well marked within the Indian populace by their names, their dress, and their distinctive temples. Moreover, we have also seen how the refusal of nationalist leaders to compromise centralized power or live up to the promises made to Sikhs during the independence movement set the stage for a long and enduring political conflict, one in which even so "secular" a leader as Nehru was not above classifying the Sikhs as a criminal tribe. This type of dehumanization was only further accentuated under his daughter, Indira Gandhi, who readily labeled the Sikhs as "secessionists" in an elaborate ploy to consolidate her support among Hindus in Punjab and divide the Sikh vote between the supposed moderates of Akali Dal and the supposed extremists of Bhindrawale (Van Dyke 1996, 216). Once the Hindu-led Indian state realized that Bhindranwale had become too popular to control, and too principled to compromise on the demands of the Anandpur Resolution, the only possible course of action was direct violence to eliminate him and the Sikh population in general. This is well-evidenced not only in the direct military action that occurred but also in the manner in which the Congress party and government officials organized and licensed the anti-Sikh massacres. It is telling that reports in the aftermath of Indira Gandhi's assassination stated that "meetings were held on the night of October 31 by Congress officials, pulling together their previously made plans to 'exterminate the Sikhs,'" and that following the riots police were even said to have chastised Hindu rioters for their lack of initiative: "We gave you 36 hours. Had we given the Sikhs that much time they would have killed every Hindu" (Van Dyke 1996, 207 & 210).

What is perhaps most disturbing and disconcerting, however, is the final genocidal component that accompanied the events of 1984: denial. The Indian State has consistently denied that it engaged in any systematic attempt to exterminate the Sikh population despite the events being marked by a persistent gap between official discourse and reality. From the "secessionist" label applied to the Sikhs before 1984, the rumors and lies that were circulated during the anti-Sikh massacres, or the official denials and distortions that followed, the Indian State appears to have perfectly followed those stages of genocide presented by Stanton. As anthropologist Linda Green suggests, "terror's power… is exactly about doubting one's own perceptions of reality" (Green 1994, 231). More than any of the gruesome killings that occurred, it is this form of terror that pervades the events of 1984, creating a dissonant reality between the lived experiences and memories of the Sikh community, and the Indian state's attempt to dissimulate, distort, and misrepresent that reality.

June: Operation Blue Star

In a memoir published following his death, the governor of Punjab during the 1984 Indian Army attack, Bhairab Dutt Pande, reported Indira Gandhi's fervent contempt for the Sikh community. Recounting his first meeting with her, Pande states, "she added that she would not hesitate to bomb the Golden Temple if she had to." India's attempts to justify Operation Blue

Star prior to and after the attacks on the Sikh community demonstrate how neo-fascist ideology has rotted the very concept of democracy in India. As historian Ajmer Singh describes it, the Indian government sought to eliminate and subdue the Sikhs politically, intellectually, and culturally, systematically destroying their religious and political institutions in order to permanently control them (Singh 2009, 143). The first step in this process was the assault on the Golden Temple which killed thousands of innocent pilgrims, destroyed the most sacrosanct of Sikh religious sites and one of the most important institutions—the Akal Takht and the concept of "Miri" and "Piri," and permanently shattered Sikh trust in the Indian government.

The intentions of the Indian government leading up to the attack were evident: BD Pande reports that a false narrative (alleging economic downturn, extremist violence, and terrorist threats) about Punjab was constructed in the months prior to Operation Blue Star in order to dehumanize and alienate the Sikh community, as well as justify military action (Pande 2021, 235). By contrast, Pande finds a very different picture of the situation of Punjab: the state's economy and industrial production had been increasing "as evidenced by larger sales tax revenues and increased octroi income of the bigger municipal corporations" (ibid). Yet the Indian State "would not accept this as it went against their preconceived notion that Punjab must be badly off—every activity must be disrupted" (ibid). In fact, Pande goes on to say that at the time of the attack, Punjab had the highest per capita income among the states of India, and that the disinformation campaign on the situation of the region was mostly carried out by the Hindu-owned national press (which had close ties with the Indian state). Thus, a nation-wide narrative was constructed to deliberately amplify conflict and tension in the Punjab region, providing material for Indian reactionaries and neo-fascists within the government to advocate for extreme methods of violent intervention."What was considered to be a normal crime in other states became terrorist and secessionist activity in Punjab" (Pande 2021, 266). This depiction of the Sikh community as a national threat targeting the common people took a significant toll on the relationship between the Sikhs and the broader Indian population, most especially with the Hindus, who had been largely convinced that the Sikhs were dangerous separatists. As Dr. Kepley Mahmood reported, "I... saw personally what was happening to the totally uninvolved and apolitical Sikhs I know. They were stopped and searched before going into movie theaters for fear they might be carrying bombs. Hindu shopkeepers with whom they had always dealt suddenly refused to serve them" (Mehmood 1997, 83). The carefully constructed web of narratives that the Indian government had woven easily ensnared ordinary people and led to a spiraling escalation of tensions between groups. When Sikhs began to arm themselves in response to Hindu flash mobs and lynchings, this was naturally interpreted as terrorist and secessionist activity, which immediately placed the Sikhs amidst the crosshairs of a genocidal Indian government and provided the justification for further persecution.

Despite tensions that spelled an imminent civil war, Prime Minister Gandhi continued to denounce Sikh leaders of the Anandpur Resolution movement as terrorists with little effort to de-escalate. Pande even alleges that offers of negotiation and peace were simply based upon false pretenses and that Indira Gandhi had no real desire to achieve peace—perhaps seeking to extend her declaration of emergency powers (which granted her nearly unchecked authority over India) through conflict: "It is true that the Prime Minister continued to say that the doors for negotiations were always open. Some clandestine talks were also going on. But mainly the purpose of these was to divert attention" (Pande 2021, 271-272). On the other hand, Jarnail Singh Bhindranwale never raised the demand for Khalistan or went beyond his advocacy of the Anandpur Sahib Resolution. He himself was prepared for negotiations to the very end, repeatedly and publicly inviting Indira Gandhi to come to the Akal Takht for peace talks.

Thus, the military attacks and genocide seem inevitable in the face of such an extreme political and social climate. Such evidence also flies in the face of India's denial and its classification of the 1984 Sikh genocide as simply spontaneous "riots" due to the assassination of the Prime Minister by the Sikhs. Dr. Mahmood notes the carefully constructed narratives built by reactionary right-wing Hindu media aided by the Indian government as well, writing: "There is no doubt that an entire apparatus of fear dissemination worked to convince India that the Sikhs were to be distrusted. And by and large, it succeeded."

In a multifaceted and calculated operation to destroy the Sikh culture and its institutions and subdue the survivors into assimilating into Hindu culture, the Indian military stormed and looted the Golden Temple Complex along with 39 other Gurdwaras under the guise of combating terrorism. Citing the existence of weapons within "holy places," the Indian government attempted to justify their attacks on the very heart of the Sikh community, blatantly ignoring the long-standing historical fact that the Sikhs have always been an armed and perpetually prepared force. In fact, weapons within Sikh places of worship are not only tolerated but encouraged and practiced extensively. As Joyce Pettigrew astutely points out, "the army went into [the Golden Temple] not to eliminate a political figure or a political movement but to suppress the culture of people, to attack their heart, to strike a blow at their spirit and self-confidence."

Pettigrew's analysis is quite accurate, as the martyrdom day of the Sikh's fifth Guru (also the architect of the Golden Temple)—one of the holiest days for the Sikhs—was chosen for the attack on the Golden Temple. The only possible rationale for such a move is that the State sought to inflict the greatest possible number of casualties. Resistance from within the complex was crushed using tanks, armored vehicles, helicopter gunships, heavy artillery, and specialized troops. As reported by the Christian Science Monitor on the 8th of June, "for five days Punjab has been cut off from the rest of the world. There is a 24-hour curfew. All telephone and telex lines are cut. No foreigners are permitted entry and on Tuesday all Indian journalists were expelled. There are no newspapers, no trains, no buses—not even a bullock cart can move." Consequently, the only official information at the time regarding the operation flowed directly from the government, and further details from humanitarian workers and organizations would not be released until the conclusion of Operation Blue Star. Orders to shoot on sight were widely carried out. The entirety of Punjab, including its 5000 villages and 50 major cities, was converted into a concentration camp. Thousands of innocent civilians were mercilessly killed in the army's advance within the temple complex, and thousands more were murdered after the military captured the entirety of the complex. The assault on the Golden Temple complex was taken by the Sikh community not only in immediate but in deeply historical terms. It resonated with other events in the past (namely from Mughal and Afghan times) in which enemies attacked, laid siege to, and destroyed the sanctum sanctorum. As Dr. Mahmood accurately describes, "[the Sikh] community has always had a pervasive awareness of history and the role of the Sikhs in it. Sikhism is after all a very young religion, and the lives of the major figures in it are not shadowy legends but matters of the historical record." It is critical to note in the analysis of the events of 1984 that the historical persecution and harassment of the Sikh community were not shrouded in mystery or clouded by doubt on the Indian subcontinent. The trials and tribulations experienced by the Sikhs are well-known affairs of modern Indian history, and so the attack on the Golden Temple immediately drew parallels with other historical attacks.

On June 2nd, Sikh families visited the Golden Temple, as the next day marked the martyrdom of Guru Arjan Dev, the fifth Guru of the Sikhs. The calm and tranquility were only superficial, as the army made active preparations to break the peace. Recounting the experiences of two Sikhs on that day, the Citizens of Democracy reports:

> Kanwaljit Singh and Majit Singh from Delhi visited the Golden Temple and found that there was no restriction for pilgrims to enter Amritsar [the city] or even the Temple. But the exit doors... were being closed. After visiting the Temple, when Kanwaljit went at noon to the Amritsar Railway Station to catch a train for Delhi, they were told that the last train had already left and that the [train] in the evening would not be leaving. In fact, they were told that all outgoing trains had been canceled. (Nanavati 2005, 58)

Though no formal curfew was implemented, visitors were permitted to enter the Temple complex; all those who left the Golden Temple on the night of June 2nd were taken into custody. The innocent victims within the complex had yet to realize the sinister plan of the Indian officials. The same report also stated:

> Punjab had been sealed. Amritsar had been sealed. The Golden Temple had been sealed. Thousands of pilgrims and hundreds of Akali [Sikh political party] workers had been allowed to collect inside the Temple complex. They had been given no inkling or warning either of the sudden curfew or of the imminent Army attack. It was to be a... tragedy, not out of forgetfulness but out of deliberate planning and design. (Nanavati 2005, 59)

Under the guise of combating terrorism, the Indian army was to launch an attack on not only the Golden Temple but dozens of other Sikh Gurdwaras at the same time. In an interview with the Citizens of Democracy, one woman trapped within the

Temple during the attack described her companions: "Inside the [Golden Temple itself] there were about 50 to 60 persons - some granthis [priests], ragis [singers], sevadars [employees], the rest of them yatris [pilgrims and visitors] like me and my family. I did not see any armed terrorist." To this day, the Indian government maintains that Operation Blue Star was a counterterrorism campaign while independent human rights organizations have found no evidence of any terrorist threats.

On June 4th, the Army began firing upon the Golden Temple using machine guns and heavy artillery. In keeping with the fundamental principles of the faith, there was some resistance from within the complex in response to the attack. As one witness trapped within the complex during the time of the attack stated:

At about 4 am... [the attack] started with a 25-pounder [cannon ball] which fell in the ramparts of the [entrance gateway] to the left of Akal Takht with such a thunder that for a few moments I thought that the whole complex had collapsed... As we were on the first floor, and our quarter was open on all sides, our position was very vulnerable. The bullets hit our quarters on all sides and some of them pierced through the doors and landed inside the room. To add to our miseries the power and water supplies had been cut. Through a slit in the shutter of a window we saw a large number of dead bodies in the Parikarma [pathway surrounding the Temple] of the Golden Temple. They included women and children. (Nanavati 2005, 59)

Unfortunately, stories such as these that contain the vivid memories of a day of betrayal by the Indian State are far too abundant. Hundreds of Sikhs, anxious for acknowledgement and justice from their nation, raised their voices, only for their stories to fall on deaf ears. As one witness recounted his experience during the attack: "There was an approximately 1-year-old child. He was laying on top of his mother, crying and looking for milk... Two army men came, one held him up from his legs and the other hit him with the butt of the rifle in his head, and the child died on the spot" (Thali 1984). Harcharan Singh Ragi, a singer at the Temple, recounted his experience of escaping the army attack: "As we were coming out, we saw that hundreds of people were being shot down as they came out. We saw many women being shot dead by the commanders. I also would have been, but for my little girl... rushing to the Army Commander and begging to save her father's life" (Rao 1986, 70). A student trapped within the temple complex at the time shares her own observations: "There was a man lying dead. I had to place my foot on him. My foot sometimes touched somebody's hand, sometimes somebody's body. I had to move in this fashion" (Roa 1986, 69). Bhan Singh (another witness within the complex at the time) remembers "many young people aged between 18 and 22 years were killed... A lady carrying a child of only a few months saw her husband lying before her. The child was also killed on account of the firing. It was a very touching scene when she placed the dead body of the child alongside her husband's body"(Rao 1986, 69).

Meanwhile, according to another witness within the complex, "helicopter[s] hovered above and continued to fire... some of these helicopters also guided... squads of the Army by making a circle of light around the targets. Immediately after these circles, the cannon ball [artillery shell] would land on the target causing havoc. We saw a large number of boys blown to pieces" (Rao 1986, 61). The war-like tactics employed by the Indian government were undeniably disproportionate to any perceived "threat" from within the Golden Temple Complex, where thousands of innocent civilians were trapped. Those captured were forced to sit on the burning marble pathways as soldiers told them to drink the mixture of blood and urine on the ground when they begged for water. Brahma Chellany, an Associated Press correspondent who managed to remain in Amritsar after all the other journalists were escorted out, records the shooting in cold blood of Sikhs who had been taken prisoner, their hands tied behind their backs with their turbans (he was later charged with sedition) (Mahmood 1997, 94).

An employee of the Golden Temple, Prithpal Singh, corroborates Chellany's findings, describing his treatment at the hands of the Indian Army:

The Army people came to the Rest House. They tore off all my clothes, stripped me naked, my kirpan [article of faith] was snatched, my [turban] was untied to tie up my hands behind my back. They caught me by my hair and took me along with five others - who were all pilgrims - to the ruins of the water tank; there we were made to stand in a line all naked for an hour or so; we were told, "don't move or you'll be shot." They kept hitting us with the rifle butts. Then a Major came and ordered a soldier, shoot them... Six of us were in a line facing the Major when a... soldier started shooting from one end, killing four of us. (Nanavati 2005, 67)

According to Bhan Singh: "[the Army] treated the inmates of the Complex as enemies and whenever there was any person wounded on account of the firing, no Red Cross people were allowed to enter, rather the Red Cross personnel had been detained [more than a kilometer away from the main entrance to the Golden Temple]" (Rao 1986, 61). Outside the temple, army troops were on a barbaric rampage, killing and looting the surrounding houses owned by Sikhs. Denied medical aid, food, and water, the Sikhs inside the complex were slaughtered, while those who survived suffered lifelong injuries and trauma.

Second-hand accounts of the events corroborate the experiences of the survivors:

The curfew was released on June 7 and one person who had been able to escape the cordon around the Golden Temple came straggling into our village. He had come on foot, and he started telling us gruesome stories about what had happened inside. It was just like the raid by Ahmed Shah Abdali [perpetrator of the second Sikh Genocide of 1762]. Small children of only a few months old were tossed around and then killed with the butts of the rifles. Women were raped inside the sacred precincts of the Golden Temple. The army was shooting people down right and left, militants or pilgrims, it didn't matter to them. I later heard the same stories from other eyewitnesses. But little of this came out in the press. (Mahmood 1997, 185)

An elder of a Punjabi village wrote a letter to the President of India, Zail Singh, with another horrific story:

The army locked up sixty pilgrims in that room [of the hostel] and shot not only the door but the window also. Electric supply was disconnected. The night between June 5th and June 6th was extremely hot. The locked-in young men felt very thirsty after some time, and loudly knocked on the door from inside to ask the army men on duty for water. They got abuses in return, but no water. The door was not opened. Feeling suffocated and extremely thirsty, the men inside began to faint and otherwise suffer untold misery. The door of the room was opened at 8 am on June 6th. By the time fifty-five out of sixty had died. The remaining five were also semi-dead. (Mahmood 1997, 82)

Different accounts claim varying amounts of casualties, though many independent sources estimate between 7,000 and 8,000. Because the press was barred from Punjab during the Operation, a reliable estimate does not exist. Nevertheless, the clear conclusion emerges that thousands of people were killed during the Army action on the Golden Temple, a fact that the Indian government refuses to acknowledge to this day. As the Citizens of Democracy summarizes succinctly:

It was indeed a mass massacre mostly of innocents. The post-mortem reports speak of the Army's brutalities in very clear terms:

i) Most of the dead bodies had their hands tied behind their backs implying that they had not died during the action, but like… Prithipal Singh's temporary companions lined up before the firing squad, all of them must have been shot after being captured alive.

ii) At the time of the post-mortem, the bodies were in a putrid and highly decomposed state—they had been brought for post-mortem after 72 hours implying the totally callous attitude towards the injured and the dead. (Rao 1986, 76)

It is crucial to recognize that the purpose of Operation Blue Star was multifaceted and multilayered; one of the primary motivations for the Indian army's attack was the destruction of the Sikh institutions discussed in Chapter 1. In fact, Pranab Mukherjee, then Finance Minister and later President of India, right-hand man of Indira Gandhi, commented to the media that the 1984 attack on the Golden Temple gave strength to Hindu chauvinism (Singh 2009, 121). The Akal Takht, considered the political seat of authority of the Sikhs nation, was bombed and destroyed. The Sikh flag, a crucial symbol of sovereignty, was replaced with the Indian tricolor to demonstrate that the Sikh community was not, in fact, independent, but rather a subsection of Hindu-majority India. Other Gurdwaras, attacked during Operation Blue Star and afterward, were either destroyed or defiled in an attempt to humiliate and degrade the Sikh community. The langar service (community kitchens) provided by Gurdwaras were placed under the control of the State authorities to convey the message that Sikh institutions could only run at the mercy of the Indian government. Arguably most devastating of all, the Sikh Reference Library was looted and destroyed. The repository of over 1500 invaluable rare manuscripts, including original handwritten copies of religious texts and portraits were never recovered following the military invasion. Sikh organizations have alleged that the troops raided the library, loading priceless artifacts into gunny bags on military trucks and transporting them to the make-shift army camp nearby. The evidence overwhelmingly points to not a simple "counter-terrorism operation" as claimed by the Indian government, but to a careful, thorough, systematic effort to eradicate the Sikh community and destroy the very institutions that preserve its uniqueness. Milan Kundera, in his work *The Book of Laughter and Forgetting*, wrote:

> *The first step in liquidating a people is to erase its memory. Destroy its books, its culture, its history. Then have somebody write new books, manufacture a new culture, invent a new history. Before long that nation will begin to forget what it is and what it was… The struggle of man against power is the struggle of memory against forgetting. (Kundera 175)*

The 1984 army attack on the Golden Temple complex was a major first step in the Indian government's multi-year campaign to erase the Sikh community from the nation in favor of a homogenous Hindu population. Catalyzed by the growing demand by the Sikh community for a more autonomous Punjab, as was originally promised at the founding of India, the state's vicious crusade destroyed hundreds of historic temples and crippled an entire generation of Sikhs. From the very beginning of the autonomous movement in 1982, hundreds of young Sikh men were kidnapped, tortured, and illegally imprisoned (dozens continue to be held to this day). The Citizens of Democracy states:

> *[H]undreds of young men were tortured to death and reported killed in fake "encounters". Thousands were sent home from police interrogations as cripples… Sikh women were stripped and paraded in the streets and raped at police stations by police officials. To top it all, the victims were referred to as "terrorists" in government reports and the press. (Rao 1986, 42)*

The government, working in tandem with the press and extremist Hindu organizations, fabricated a narrative to defame the Sikhs and discredit their calls for greater autonomy. This narrative was then used to justify and enable human rights violations at the local and national levels. During the attack itself, the Citizens of Democracy report continues:

> *A number of responsible men and women who were inside the*
> *Golden Temple throughout the Army Action described to us*
> *how innocent people were slaughtered like rats—first letting*
> *them enter the Complex and then declaring the curfew which*
> *prevented them from going out—thousands were caught*
> *unaware; finally when the survivors were asked to surrender*
> *they were shot in cold blood... the hands of men were tied at*
> *their back with their own turbans, some of whom were shot. The*
> *post-mortem reports show how the bullets had pierced their*
> *bodies. The eyewitnesses described the use of gas by the Army,*
> *the pile of dead bodies on the [path surrounding Golden*
> *Temple], the arrival of tanks which some... thought were the*
> *ambulance, the hovering of helicopters at night, throwing their*
> *searchlight on targets which were bombed, the wanton*
> *destruction of the Akal Takht and Research Library and*
> *Museum. (Rao 1986, 10)*

The Indian army's repeated claim that Operation Blue Star
was a necessary counter-terrorism measure is a provably false
and poorly defended lie—one that has certainly left a deep scar
on the Sikh psyche. Following the military invasion, Hazara
Singh Vadle, an employee of the SGPC (the organization
charged with the management of Gurdwaras throughout the
Indian states of Punjab, Haryana, Himachal Pradesh, and union
territory Chandigarh) echoed a common sentiment in the Sikh
community: "The way the government... attacked the Golden
Temple reminded us of the medieval times when our religion
was attacked and we [were] persecuted. Thousands of women,
children, and pilgrims had gathered here on June 3 [for the
martyrdom day of the 5th Guru]. They had no connection with
politics, why [were] they shot down?" (Rao 1986, 84)

The evidence collected by international human rights
organizations regarding Operation Blue Star provides context
to the unquantifiable and unjustifiable killing during the Army,

but the exact number of victims remains unclear. According to Professor Virk of Guru Nanak University, "Death certificates were not given and no list was published of those killed in the Operation. Dead bodies were thrown in dirty refuse trucks and there was mass cremation" (Rao 1986, 19). To this day, the Indian government itself has not identified the bodies of those who died in the attack or offered compensation to affected families. Another member of the SGPC, comparing Operation Blue Star to a similar attack by the British in 1919 (known as Jallianwala Bagh), "after the Jallianwara Bagh massacre, the British government identified those killed, handed over their bodies to the next kin and paid Rs. 2000 as compensation for every person killed in the incident. Whereas in [the] Blue Star Operation, the present government... have not only not identified those killed or missing, rather they are harassing and persecuting the families and friends of those who are reportedly missing" (Rao 1986, 85).

This blatant disregard, lack of recognition, and lack of judiciary action in regards to the heinous crimes committed by the Indian government since 1984 have permanently destroyed any trust the Sikh community held for their nation. Shri Kirapal Singh's sorrowful words about the military operation are worth quoting: "When General Dyer [British officer] killed people in Jallianwala Bagh, the bodies had been given back to their relatives but strangely our own Army killed our own people and did not return the bodies to their relatives. Thereafter, a reign of terror was let loose in this area. Any Sikh youth who wore a yellow or blue turban or had a kirpan was captured, humiliated, and shot" (Rao 1986, 31). The Sikh genocide was not simply limited to a spontaneous military attack on a revered site; it was a carefully planned and executed operation consisting of months of preparation, including the conduction of military training exercises in a full-scale replica of the Golden Temple.

When painting the picture of the "Punjab Situation" of June

1984, the Indian government and media will often portray requests for greater autonomy as calls to violent and separatist action. There was, in fact, no such call for separatism—in fact, the leaders of the protests had explicitly stated that they were not in any way requesting a separate Sikh state, but rather requesting the fulfillment of the terms established at the founding of the country. For the Indian army to march into one of the holiest Sikh temples and destroy historical buildings and institutions, loot priceless manuscripts, and viciously murder thousands is not an event that the Sikh community is likely to forget (regardless of the constant propaganda that suggests to the contrary). In an attempt to destroy the very foundations of Sikhism and shatter any political movements in support of greater autonomy for Punjab, Indira Gandhi and her administration have only strengthened the separatist movements and further legitimized the case for an independent Sikh homeland.

June to October: Operation Woodrose

Immediately following the 1984 massacre in the Golden Temple complex, the Indian government significantly ramped up its mopping-up operation, codenamed "Operation Woodrose," which was begun simultaneously with Operation Blue Star. Another military action disguised as a counterterrorism initiative, Operation Woodrose extended throughout the rural villages of Punjab, targeting innocent civilians and permanently traumatizing generations of Sikhs to come. In this way, Operation Blue Star can be understood as a false flag operation designed not to target a political movement but to suppress and destroy the roots of the Sikh culture and its institutions.

Many parallels can be drawn between Operation Blue Star and Operation Woodrose such that Woodrose was in many ways simply a continuation of the work commenced in Blue Star. In both cases, state propaganda and right-wing media dehumanized the Sikh community in order to justify progressively extreme military action. Once again, Punjab was cut off from the world as the Indian Army occupied the state and wrested control of the administration. Any Sikh resistance to harassment was labeled terrorism or separatism while vague laws allowed innocent civilians to be imprisoned for indefinite amounts of time.

Much like Operation Blue Star, Woodrose was set in motion months before the killings began. However, Blue Star provided the propagandistic foundation and justification for the commencement of Woodrose. To legitimize the Army occupation, the Indian government declared Punjab and Chandigarh as "disturbed areas" in the Punjab Chandigarh Disturbed Area Act of 1983, essentially declaring the entire state of Punjab as hostile enemy territory. In Ajit Ram Darshi's analysis of the operation, "the main purpose of this operation was to mop up all [baptized] Sikhs, especially the young men, from the villages of Punjab. During this mopping-up operation, the Army indiscriminately picked up all the Sikh boys and other Sikhs who had... beards and... a small dagger" (Darshi 2004, 137). In the Indian Army's official publication, it was reported that all baptized Sikhs were to be considered extremists and immediately reported to the authorities, which only served to fuel the already strained relationship between Hindus and Sikhs. Post-Operation Blue Star propaganda was similarly distributed (but badly misfired). Following Blue Star, in an attempt to discredit the Sikh resistance fighters and paint them merely as opportunistic thugs, Indian authorities claimed that, in their search of the Golden Temple, a large haul of narcotics, money, and gems had been discovered. However, these statements were later recanted by the government as no such recoveries had actually been found within the complex. (Pande 2021, 277-278)

Unfortunately, the majority of anti-Sikh propaganda during Operation Woodrose was not similarly exposed and disavowed, instead creating a self-perpetuating cycle of tension and violence.

The surgically methodical process through which Operation Woodrose was executed has been well-documented by various historians and anthropologists. Though it went largely unnoticed by international governments, the bloody and brutal Operation Blue Star of June 1984 certainly garnered the attention of a smattering of human rights organizations, the social-scientific community, and, naturally, diaspora Sikhs, much to the Indian government's dismay. Indian human rights group The People's Union for Civil Liberties accused Punjab police of behaving like a "barbarian force," as Sikhs were declared criminals and held indefinitely, tortured, raped, and killed, never to be seen again (Mahmood 1997, 81). The human rights violations perpetrated by the Indian government were documented by Amnesty International, including scores of "disappearances," extrajudicial killings, widespread torture, unacknowledged detentions as well as deaths in custody (Amnesty International 2005). The state and central governments continue to deny the occurrence of virtually all these violations.

As Mary Anne Weaver describes in her eye-opening account:

The pattern in each village appears to be the same. The Army moves in during the early evening, cordons a village, and announces over loudspeakers that everyone must come out. All males between the ages of 15 and 35 are trussed and blindfolded, then taken away... [at local Gurdwaras], worshippers and temple workers [are blindfolded] and pushed with rifle butts to the narrow dirt road outside, where they were given electroshock charges with high-powered batteries attached to Army trucks. (Weaver 1984)

In his own book, Ajmer Singh continued:

Everyone was closely monitored and, if [the Army] doubted anyone even slightly, the Sikhs were immediately taken into custody. The baptized Sikhs, especially the youth, were seen through a lens of doubt and were questioned thoroughly. (Singh 2009, 137)

A.R. Darshi further elaborates on the process:

Like hunting hounds, [the Army] rounded up thousands of Sikhs, especially the youths, detained them in military camps, tortured them brutally, and in many cases shot them dead. Many were crippled and maimed permanently....... The mothers, sisters, and wives of the Sikhs who went underground for fear of arbitrary arrests, were arrested, detained in military camps, tortured and in many cases molested in order to force their fleeing relatives to surrender. There was none to hear their wails and woes; there was none to give them healing touch. (Darshi 2004, 138)

This process of arbitrarily detaining, questioning, torturing, and quietly killing, continued for about 3 months—during this time, police stations, rest houses, and army camps were converted into "interrogation centers" where the Sikhs in custody were tortured and "disappeared."

One particular whistleblower exposé to examine is the Citizens of Democracy report, which gathered hundreds of firsthand accounts regarding the 1984 events. Banned in India, it detailed multiple bone-chilling reports of a McCarthy-style witch-hunt, sadistic torture, and cold-blooded shooting of young baptized Sikh men, along with rape and violence perpetrated against women. Sukhdev Singh, a villager who witnessed the events of Woodrose firsthand, explained, "for every 1 member

of a family missing or detained members of 20 other families
would be harassed and troubled in every conceivable way and
their crops would be destroyed" (Rao 1986, 49). Many rural
incidents in which young Sikh men would be detained involved
what were contemptuously known as "pen-knife" cases. As
Citizens of Democracy reported, "revolvers and pistols were
sometimes planted on the boys; even one cartridge would do
the job. One of these 'extremists' holding up his tattered banyan,
asked us 'where could I have hidden the revolver?'" (Rao 1986,
11). In order to avoid such fates, thousands of young Sikh men
went underground, living a nomadic lifestyle in the wilderness.
Those who were caught would never be heard from again, as
was the case with Sohan Singh:

> Sohan Singh's eyes had been gouged out, every joint of his body
> had been broken with steel rods; later when his body was handed
> over to his widow and his elder brother Baldev Singh, they
> found the eyes were not there, and the body was just a pulp
> without joints and it had become unusually long. The Army
> had handed the body over to police, which was entered as a case
> of suicide. The widow was made to sign a statement that it was
> a case of suicide; there was no post-mortem to prove that the
> man had died of torture. (Rao 1986, 30)

In an interview with a Sikh militant, Cynthia Keppley
Mahmood records "One man I interviewed had just gotten out
of India a month before I met him, and in the intervening time,
his wife and infant son had been arrested. Police apparently tied
the child to a block of ice in order to make this militant's wife
tell them where he was. Rather than succumbing to the
temptation to try to spare her child, she asked for a glass of water
and when it arrived, she smashed it on the desktop and slit her
throat with the ragged edge. She died on the spot" (Mahmood
1997, 202).

According to Dr. Sangat Singh, who served on the Joint
Intelligence Committee, about 100,000 Sikh youth had been

taken into custody within the first four to six weeks of Operation Woodrose, adding that many of them were not heard from again. He further states that about 20,000 youth crossed over the border to Pakistan (Singh 2014, 384). According to estimates published by historian Inderjit Singh Jaijee, approximately 1 million individuals were reported as missing or killed as a result of Army operations during this period (Jaijee 1999, 216). Unfortunately, it is impossible to pinpoint exactly how many Sikhs were killed, as the Indian government kept no records of the killings and simply cremated the bodies or threw them into mass graves. In summarizing, the Citizens of Democracy reported: "if some, unable to bear the torture, die, no postmortem is called for, since there is no record of their arrest; even the bodies are not handed over; if in some case they are, the relative taking over the body has to certify under the threat of being shot down that the man had committed suicide" (Rao 1986, 29).

Although the initial campaign for greater autonomy and rights in Punjab was unrelated to the notion of an independent Sikh country, the unstoppable tide of violence and harassment against innocent civilians naturally led many to question their place in India. According to historian Ajmer Singh, it quickly became clear that the extermination of the Sikhs in the name of counterterrorism was not simply state repression of the common people, but was directed specifically towards the Sikhs (Singh 2009, 143). The realization by the community that the Sikhs would forever be second-class citizens is precisely what led to the growing support for "Khalistan," a separate Sikh homeland free of persecution. To this day, the impact of not only Operation Blue Star but the sanguinary months that followed reverberates throughout the Sikh community as thousands continue to await justice.

November: The Sikh Pogroms

On October 31st, 1984, Indian Prime Minister Indira Gandhi, who was largely responsible for the execution of Operation Blue Star and Woodrose, was assassinated by her Sikh bodyguards. Naturally, the question arises of her maintenance of Sikh security despite Operation Blue Star, a military action that turned nearly the entirety of the Sikh community against Gandhi. However, the presence of Sikh bodyguards was in fact a political stunt by the Prime Minister to demonstrate to the people that despite the bloody Blue Star, she still held the approval of the community and was unafraid of any potential treachery on their part. In spite of her fascist and partisan policies, Indira Gandhi continued to enjoy the favor of the Hindu community, particularly right-wing members, while also continuing to alienate minority-religious groups. Clearly, her assumption and reliance on the Sikh community's loyalty were sorely misguided, but her assassination held grave consequences for the future of the Sikhs.

Immediately following Gandhi's assasination, November commenced with a series of organized pogroms against the Sikhs, particularly those concentrated outside of the Punjab region. According to Paul Brass,: "it is past time to note that Indian politics and society display many of the symptoms of a murderous pre-fascist stage which has already produced a multiplicity of localized Kristallnachts in numerous urban sites" (Mahmood 1997, 138). Similarly, Khushwant Singh, an author, politician, and recipient of the Padma Bhushan award—one of the highest Indian civilian awards—told a commission, "I felt like a refugee in my own country. In fact, I felt like a Jew in Nazi Germany"(Shrivastava 2005). Though some will undoubtedly find these analogies with Nazi Germany here too extreme, both the explicit targeting of baptized Sikhs following Operation Blue

Star and the clear earmarking of Sikh residences and businesses speak to a genocidal campaign.

The attacks on the Golden Temple and subsequent hunting of Sikh youth in the street of Punjab quickly blossomed into the lynchings of Sikhs throughout India. The brutal killing, looting, and raping of Sikh citizens spread through the Indian states and territories of Delhi, Jharkhand, Madhya Pradesh, Haryana, Uttarakhand, Bihar, Uttar Pradesh, West Bengal, Himachal Pradesh, Rajasthan, Orissa, Jammu & Kashmir, Chattisgarh, Tripura, Tamil Nadu, Gujarat, Andhra Pradesh, Kerala and Maharashtra (Sikh Press Associates 2019). Sikhs were assaulted by rage-fueled Hindu extremist mobs; government officials reported that these mobs were often assisted by the military or local police, who had collected voter registration lists of Sikhs (which included names, ages, and addresses) and distributed them amongst the groups while supplying them with iron rods and gasoline (Van Dyke 1996). Union Secretary BD Pande reported that "Hindu communalists were being helped by the Congress [political party of Indira Gandhi] circles in Delhi and elsewhere" (Pande 2021, 260). In a secret meeting held at 24 Akbar Road, New Delhi on October 31, 1984, Parliament officials and senior Congress party members, including Jagdish Tytler, Sajjan Kumar, Kamal Nath, Dharam Das Shastri, Vasant Sathe, HKL Bhagat, Lalit Makhen, and Arjun Das, amongst others, were reported planning the massacre of Sikhs.

In the sustenance of the Sikh genocide, government institutions—particularly those with military force—played an instrumental role, without which such a longstanding massacre could not have been organized, executed, and subsequently ignored. However, state-sponsored media and propaganda also played an instrumental role, which is often overlooked in such analyses of genocides. In the case of the events of 1984, state media showed inflammatory speeches and scenes calling for the criminalization and murder of Sikhs. Popular movie stars like

Amitabh Bachchan were depicted on state television channels raising slogans such as "blood for blood" and "splashes of blood should reach the doorsteps of the Sikhs," only fueling the already vengeful extremists (Voice Online 2014). Following such calls to action, local police often assisted mobs in locating, disarming, and killing innocent Sikhs. Detailing the methods often utilized by the Indian police in Sikh areas, Joyce Pettigrew noted: "No protection came from the police. Indeed, the police first seized the licensed weapons of the Sikh inhabitants of these areas and, the Sikhs disarmed, the mobs were free to enter" (Pettigrew 1995, 9).

Once they were granted full access to the exact whereabouts of the Sikhs in every area, the mobs were free to prowl the streets, hunting, beating, and burning any Sikh in sight. However, it is not to be interpreted that these killings were random occurrences by grief-struck supporters of Indira Gandhi—November constituted a systematic and thoroughly-planned attack on the psyche of the Sikh community. In the trans-Jumna area of Delhi, neighborhoods were surrounded and their Sikh inhabitants were burnt alive (Pettigrew 1995, 9). While Sikh homes and businesses were looted and irrecoverably destroyed, neighboring structures stayed intact. Sikhs were beaten to death, "necklaced" with tires and soaked in kerosene and set afire, dismembered, and raped (Mahmood 1997, 138). Police officers were reported supplying the gasoline and metal rods, directing mobs to Sikh places of residence, refusing to assist those who managed to flee to police stations, and suppressing any Sikh resistance to the gangs. One woman, who witnessed the attacks firsthand, reported:

People were on fire, literally on fire - one man's turban had gotten kerosene poured on it, and he became a human torch. I saw another man leap off a roof, and flames... followed his body in a big arc, like a shooting star. And the thing that I will never forget was the way those Sikh bodies on fire were shaking, trembling, as they burned. That driver in my car turned to his companion and said, "See, they are dancing bhangra [a Punjabi folk dance]..." later it became clear that it wasn't just this driver, it was everybody. No one cared about the Sikhs. We had been deluding ourselves all this time, that we were instrumental to the nation, that people respected us. (Mahmood 1997, 137)

This perfectly summarizes the Sikh community's sense of betrayal and anguish. Not only were religious places attacked and destroyed, with thousands of innocent Sikhs massacred inside, but the safety of homes and villages was threatened shortly thereafter as extremist mobs ran rampant and untouched through the streets of India. Harji Malik, a journalist with the Hindustan Times, visited one of the areas worst hit by the carnage, Trilokpuri Block 32, nearly a year after the anti-Sikh massacres, and described the continuing aura of devastation poignantly:

This infamous block where the massacre of men and boys had been most savage, had not been touched for almost a year. No family had returned and it was easy to see why. Burned out houses, charred door frames, piles of rubble, heaps of half-burned clothes, a child's rubber [sandal], charred paper obviously used to light fires, heaps of ashes inside ruined rooms, remained mute witnesses to man's brutality. From the walls of many stricken homes painted plaques of Guru Nanak looked down on the evidence of human madness. The narrow street, both sides lined with gutted shells of homes, exuded its own horrors, its desolation a stark contrast to the overcrowded streets, bustling with life, on either side. In block 32 the silence speaks, for pain and agony have been permanently recorded here. (Mahmood 1997, 141)

Given countless testimonials, dozens of human rights organizations, and millions of Sikhs worldwide, it is impossible to conclude that the events of 1984 were anything short of a deliberate, systematic attempt by the Indian government to eradicate, if not the entire population, at least an entire generation of young Sikhs largely responsible for the movement in favor of a more autonomous Punjab. Indira Gandhi's son and ascending Prime Minister, Rajiv Gandhi, in a shocking justification of the state-sanctioned genocidal massacres, commented, "when a great tree shakes, the earth trembles" (Pettigrew 1995, 9). The government's casual disregard for the lives of the Sikhs, simply dismissing the massacres as spontaneous, unsanctioned riots blatantly flies in the face of democracy and the supposed "secularism" of the nation. The Citizens Justice Commission, headed by former Chief Justice S.M. Sikri, which included a former governor, former commonwealth secretary, and a former union home secretary, concluded that the anti-Sikh violence was a "massive, deliberate, planned onslaught on the life, property, and honor of a comparatively small, but easily identifiable, minority community" (Mahmood 1997, 138). In 1984, the Sikh community, as a religious and political group, was attacked on three successive occasions. On each of those occasions, their social class, family background, service to, and positions in the State structures were automatically negated as a simple consequence of their cultural identity, removing their rights and dignity from them.

In summary, official records reported that over 3000 Sikhs were killed, while human rights and independent organizations indicate that over 30,000 were murdered and 200,000 were displaced (Nanavati 2005; Pillalamarri 2014; Mukhoty and Kothari 1984). Sikhs seen on public roads were burnt alive, dragged from trains, and hanged or set alight. Millions of dollars in Sikh-owned property were looted and destroyed. Roughly 300 Sikh soldiers were murdered in uniform. In the state of Jharkhand, 120 Sikhs working in the Bokaro Steel Plant were thrown alive into burning furnaces. In Jabalpur, a city in the state of Madhya Pradesh, 12 Sikhs were hung from the ceiling of a railway platform. In the city of Agartala, 40 Sikh families who took refuge in a police station to save their lives were burnt alive in the station. In Haryana and Madhya Pradesh, Sikh women were taken hostage and held captive as sex slaves. Even after November, it was common for refugee camps to be raided and Sikh women kidnapped and raped. Hundreds of Sikh women were gang-raped throughout India by Hindu mobs, police officers, and civil administrators. A common taunt at the time was that the next generation (the children of the Sikh women and their Hindu rapists) would be loyal to the government. Children as young as 13 days of age were roasted alive on gas stoves in Kanpur. Toddlers were ruthlessly murdered as mobs tore them limb from limb while their mothers were raped in front of them. While the official position of the Indian government is that the "anti-Sikh riots" were simply a result of disorganized chaos in which Sikhs were targeted simply due to their association with the assassins of Indira Gandhi, the highly efficient, specific nature of the attacks are representative of greater governmental involvement in the genocidal campaign, one which—as we shall see in the next chapter, continued well beyond 1984 itself.

As we observed in the opening of this chapter, denial is the well-worn follow-up to almost any genocide. It is among the surest indicators of future massacres. The perpetrators of genocide dig up the mass graves, burn the bodies, try to cover up the evidence, and intimidate the witnesses. They deny that they committed any crimes, and often blame what happened to the victims or accuse them of fabricating narratives. They block investigations of the crimes and continue to govern until driven from power by force. It is this stage that is perhaps most obvious and outrageous in India as increasing evidence of atrocities is brought forth and repeatedly ignored. Even during the vicious massacres, the Hindu-run media's coverage of the events appeared apathetic at best and, more damningly, willingly abetting mass murder. Cynthia Keppley Mahmood reported the stark contrast between reality and reports:

> As Hindu mobs abetted by police slaughtered thousands of Sikhs in cities across India, this massacre was accompanied by ridicule. Sikh bodies, shaking as they burned in the streets of Delhi, were said to be "dancing the bhangra" (a Punjabi folk dance)... it was not only the sight of humans on fire that was horrific but the terrible asynchrony of this vision with ongoing radio commentary that was painting a wildly different picture... one doubted one's own perceptions... an Indian commentator said that the radio bulletins during the riots "could have been coming from another planet." (Mahmood 1997, 188)

Following the attacks on the Golden Temple, Dr. Mahmood observed:

> In the photographs that quickly made the rounds in the Sikh community, passing from hand to hand with shocked horror, was the Akal Takht with a gaping hole in its dome, its walls pockmarked with bullets, the pavement in front soaked with blood and littered with bodies. They saw the Sikh Reference Library in ashes, the rooftops of Amritsar smoking. With all of this physical destruction, however, in a way it was the Indian government's continuing denial of substantial harm that was the most psychologically damaging aspect of the entire event. (Mahmood 1997, 188)

To this day, the Indian government refuses to officially acknowledge the events of 1984, retaining that Sikhs were, and are, terrorists. Political prisoners languish in jails even after completing their sentences, and families anxiously await news regarding those who mysteriously disappeared decades ago, while murderers live freely despite overwhelming evidence of their guilt. While the lack of justice is hardly surprising, it does provide a more complete picture of India—highlighting the dark side of "the largest democracy on Earth" that is so often held up as a shining example. The appropriate response to the genocide and its subsequent denial is punishment by an international tribunal or national court. Such courts may deter future potential genocidists who may never again share Hitler's expectation of impunity when he sneered, "Who, after all, remembers the annihilation of the Armenians?" However, with a nation-state dedicated to keeping knowledge of the events hidden and the facts muddled, it falls upon the Sikh community to not only educate, but to seek justice before rushing to attempt to heal the wounds of 1984.

CONCLUSION

The Atrophy of Indian Democracy

Conclusion

The Atrophy of Indian Democracy

The events of 1984 permanently shifted the social and political dynamics of India. While the Sikh community had been no stranger to discrimination even prior to the genocide, the actions of the government and its constant validation of the right-wing Hindu majority divided the country and irreversibly scarred the Sikhs. Amandeep Kaur best summarizes how this impacted Sikh consciousness: "I realized… that there were two sets of laws in this country, one for Hindus who can hold their ceremonies anyplace they like, and another for us, who can't even commemorate the death of one of our young boys. The clear message was that this country doesn't belong to us" (Mahmood 1997, 218). In an atmosphere of deceit and denial following the assault on the Golden Temple and consequent assassination of Indira Gandhi, massacres presented themselves as assertions of hard truth. "The government wanted to kill us," one woman said incredulously, expressing this recognition (Mahmood 1997, 189). Art depicting the massacre—including vivid images of bleeding and bullet-riddled bodies lying in the foreground of the Akal Takht—was widely distributed throughout the community, becoming a constant reminder of the heinous crimes against the Sikhs. As Cynthia Keppley Mahmood describes, "Their potency derives only in part from their blood; it derives also from their unwillingness to be mashed, covered, or distorted. The slaughter is there for all to see, whatever statistics are released or policies promulgated" (Mahmood 1997, 189). Meanwhile, the Indian government's unwillingness to recognize the attack on the Golden Temple as a heinous crime, as they instead attempted to justify the actions of Indira Gandhi, served as (and continues to be) a strong warning to the Sikh community: that the Indian State does not represent or care for the existence or sentiments of the minority Sikhs.

It is unsurprising, then, that the demand for Khalistan, or a separate Sikh state, was amplified in the years following the attacks on the most revered temple of the faith. The Sikhs had realized that having failed to assimilate into the Hindu culture, they had been marked for annihilation. While the attacks were undoubtedly partially motivated by the politics of Indira Gandhi and the Congress Party, it is clear that the crux of the conflict was cultural and religious. The Sikh institutions such as the Akal Takht, concepts of "Miri," "Piri," and Langar directly clash with the foundational concepts of Hinduism and Hindustan. Seeing their very identity literally under fire, and the government labeling any baptized Sikh a terrorist, thousands of young Sikh men between the ages of 15 and 40 went underground, joining militarist organizations in the hopes of exacting their own justice for the crimes committed against their people.

While we tend to think of the Sikh genocide as largely contained between June and November of 1984, the years following were filled with secretive, Gestapo-style police and military operations that harkened back to Nazi Germany. Particularly during 1987 and 1988, it became clear that the government was organizing specialized extralegal hit squads to go after those Sikhs who had begun arming themselves, and there were hints that the functioning of these squads was approved at the highest levels of government. Sushil Muni, a Jain monk who had been working as an intermediary between the government and the Sikh militants, said outright that the government itself was fomenting terrorism in Punjab, and there were government officials who would corroborate his claims (Mahmood 1997, 158).

By the early 1990s, thousands of Sikhs, particularly young men, were unjustly arrested, tortured, and held indefinitely as political prisoners without being charged. Mahmood reports a common police tactic in which "whenever anybody is bonded out of jail a big police force is standing outside the court. Then when the prisoner is released he is immediately arrested again" (Mahmood 1997, 148). One Sikh who joined the resistance movement recounted a story of his friend, who was killed in police custody: "The way my brave friend finally died, it was horrible. When his body was discovered, he had no teeth, no nails on his hands and feet, and his chest was entirely blackened. That was how he died" (Mahmood 1997, 154). Throughout India, rampant discrimination and harassment were targeted at Sikhs at all levels of society. Amandeep Kaur, a college girl narrating her tale, said "it was paining my heart that Sikh boys and girls who were really deserving couldn't reach the positions in life they deserved. I saw discrimination everywhere" (Mahmood 1997, 214).

The extrajudicial killings and further harassment only fueled more calls from within the Sikh community for its forcible secession from the Indian State. Additionally, the Indian propaganda apparatus continued to actively label Sikhs as a threat to the very fabric of the nation, promoting Hindu unity in the face of a menacing "other". In any democracy, the press plays a critical role in upholding the sanctity of freedom and democratic principles; but in 1984, the "continuous media propaganda in the Punjab vernacular papers and even the national dailies was adding to this estrangement" (Pande 2021, 262).

Between the years 1984 to 1992, India deployed nearly 500,000 troops in Punjab alone. During that period, hundreds of thousands of Sikhs throughout the entirety of India were harassed, raped, kidnapped, tortured, murdered, and disappeared at the hands of Indian authorities. The Sikh culture and the examples set by the Gurus themselves have served as sources of inspiration for resistance movements—particularly the moral obligation of every Sikh to employ "force to restore justice in society as well as to resist in high spirits, cheerfully, and offer unyielding resistance" (Pettigrew 1995, 31). In the Sikh faith, resistance to oppression is understood as an honorable response. Throughout the genocidal process (and well after it), the government continued to produce victim-blaming propaganda in order to alienate the Sikh community and provoke militarist organizations to respond to violence with violence.

Crackdown on the Sikh Identity

Today, the very justice system of India is split, as minorities are punished significantly more harshly than those of the majority, perpetuating a corrupt and unjust system—a fact that Indian Supreme Court Justices have commented on. Journalist Arvind Verma reported, "torture is routinely practiced in most police stations and death in police custody is a frequent phenomenon," (Perry 2013, 138) while outside of jails the police practice of getting rid of suspects through staged encounters is unfortunately all too common. Indian Chief Justice Nuthalapati Ramana said that rather than being the safest places, "the threat to human rights and bodily integrity are the highest in police stations. Custodial torture and other police atrocities are problems which still prevail in our society" (Trivedi 2001). Even former Indian Supreme Court Justice Krishna Iyer stated that he would not rely on the nation's highest court to establish a fair and timely decision, as "justice in Punjab has been crucified on the cross of law" (Mahmood 1997, 99). Additionally, four Indian Supreme Court Justices, in a 2018 press conference, stated that "unless this institution is preserved and it maintains its equanimity, democracy will not survive in this country"

(Dev 2019). In a democratic society, judicial branches of government are hallowed institutions dedicated to upholding the law and order of the land. However, in India, the corruption of the justice system has been recognized by both those within and outside of the institution; consequently, the CATO Institute, in its annual Human Freedom Index, classified the fairness of the criminal justice system as a mere four out of ten.

As we have already seen, one of the primary avenues by which the Indian government disproportionately targets minority groups is through security legislation, in which Sikhs are branded as "terrorists" and threats to national security. While seemingly present in the interest of national security, these laws vest unchecked powers in the police to circumvent the due process that has been established to protect a citizen's right to a fair trial. These laws place the responsibility of proving innocence on the accused—an undeniable breach of justice—and perpetuate a "guilty until proven innocent" environment to limit the freedoms of every accused individual. In essence, they operate as preventive detention laws, unjustly criminalizing the intentions, beliefs, and thoughts of a person.

The blatant discrimination within the Indian justice system, enforced through sweeping "security" legislation, was largely aimed not to promote impartial judgement on criminals, but to appease a majority demographic convinced that the Sikh community was rife with terrorists. In the case of Kehar Singh, who was accused of conspiracy in the assassination of Indira Gandhi, the International Commission of Jurists pleaded with President Ramaswamy Venkataraman to grant clemency to the accused. In the text of the appeal, Commission Secretary-General Naill MacDermont, a British Labour Party politician, noted the repeated rejections of mercy:

The International Commission of Jurists is profoundly disturbed by the rejection of pleas for mercy which have caused deep concern among the jurists throughout the world. As appears from the judgment, the only substantial evidence on which his conviction was based was that he had talks with Beant Singh [one of the assassins] on various occasions but there was no evidence as to the contents of those talks. We beseech you to exercise your right and power to have regard to the merits of the case in order to prevent what might be a terrible error of justice. (Joshi 1984, 161)

Despite only being accused with only circumstantial evidence, Kehar Singh was convicted and executed for conspiracy.

The disparity between the treatment of Hindus and Sikhs incomparable crimes is evident in cases throughout India. For example, Sadhvi Pragya, an Indian politician, was convicted in the right-wing Hindu organization Abhinav Bharat's 2008 bomb blast in Malegaon that killed ten and injured nearly 100. However, she was released on bail in 2017 and elected as a Member of Parliament to the Bharatiya Janata Party, becoming the "face" of many Hindu nationalist movements. Similarly, Colonel Prasad Purohit, an accomplice to the same attack, was not only released but reinstated into the Army. On the other hand, Professor Devinder Pal Singh Bhullar, a Sikh, was sentenced to life in prison after being "found" guilty of killing nine and injuring 31 in a 1993 car bombing. In the evidence presented to the court, the police alleged that Bhullar volunteered a confession, which was typed on a police computer while Bhullar spoke. However, according to the authorities, the secretary forgot to save the confession on the computer. It should be noted that the Terrorist and Disruptive Activities Act (TADA) in India requires a confession to be handwritten or an audio/video record of it to be kept. In spite of such flimsy and likely fabricated evidence, Bhullar was found guilty and sentenced to death, which would later be commuted to life in prison. He remains in prison despite calls for clemency from the European Parliament, the Chief Minister of Delhi, and dozens of international organizations.

In another case, three Sikh youth were sentenced to life imprisonment merely for their possessions of books encouraging the establishment of a separate Sikh homeland. The Association for Democratic Rights called the court decision a dangerous attack on democratic freedoms. (The Tribune India 2019) The Association members said the Sikh youths were not involved in any anti-national activity or viable threats to the internal security of the nation, calling the decision a politically motivated statement with no evidence of violent action. Moreover, the very content of the books and literature in the possession of the Sikhs was not banned under the law. Such decisions dilute and degrade the democratic fundamental rights and values of the country. Under the right-wing Hindu ideology that has long dominated Indian spheres of power, writers, intellectuals, and activists (particularly those of minority backgrounds) are attacked, undermining the "democratic" system established at the founding of the country; the true nature of which is only witnessed through such violations of justice.

It is critical to note that the tactics employed against the Sikhs in this regard are by no means limited to the community, but have rather become part of an authoritarian apparatus that targets all manner of minority groups. Activists like Arun Ferreira and Vernon Gonsalves have advocated the need for a citizen's movement that questions the very premise of India's security laws including disproportionate targeting, wrongful incarceration, torture during interrogation, and the overarching infringement of fundamental rights, especially Article 19 and Article 21 of the Indian Constitution, which protect the rights to "hold opinions without interference and to seek, receive and impart information and ideas through any media and regardless of frontiers." In their report, Bhamati Sivapalan and Vidyun Sabhaney definitively state that "the misuse of security laws… is widespread" (Sivapalan and Sabhaney 2019).

Examples of the abuse of security laws outside the Sikh context include the case of Afzal Guru (not to be confused with the Sikh Gurus), a Kashmiri separatist accused of playing a role in the 2001 Indian Parliament attack. During Afzal's sentencing, the Supreme Court acknowledged that even the police charge sheet did not accuse Afzal of any charges meriting capital punishment and that the evidence was circumstantial. Following his arrest, Guru was held in a special cell and made a confessional statement that bore his signature. In the very preamble of the confession, it was recorded that the Deputy Commissioner of Police had asked policemen to leave the room. However, after seven months, Guru disowned this confession and the Supreme Court refused to accept the earlier confession as evidence against him. Journalist Vinod K. Jose claimed that in an interview in 2006, Guru had said that he had been subjected to extreme torture which included electric shocks to his genitals and being beaten up for hours along with threats regarding his family (he was told that his brother was held in detention) after his arrest. Moreover, at the time of his confession, he had no legal representation. The Supreme Court assessment stated, "as is the case with most conspiracies, there is and could be no evidence amounting to criminal conspiracy" (Sidiq 2020). However, justifying the capital punishment conviction based on circumstantial evidence, the report went on to say: "the incident, which resulted in heavy casualties, had shaken the entire nation, and the collective conscience of society will only be satisfied if capital punishment is awarded to the offender" (Duschinski et al 2018, 32). India's lack of egalitarianism within the judicial system is astounding—from the lack of fair and equal representation to the falsified confessions extracted through brutal threats and torture. Stanley Wolpert, writing in *A New History of India*, notes that "though India had signed the UN Declaration of Universal Human Rights, her legal system now clearly violated its basic provisions and left more and more of its citizens to languish behind prison bars without any stated cause for such action or real hope of freedom" (Mahmood 1997, 99).

These unjust laws, concealed and approved under the vague concept of "internal security," limit the freedoms of the individual and maximize the authoritarian powers of the State. As Sivapalan and Sabhaney summarize "at the receiving end [of these laws] are minority communities, Dalits, indigenous communities, trade unionists, those living in states with separatist movements, journalists, activists, students, and artists. Given the history of how these laws are applied and whom they are applied against, it is unlikely that the new amendments will operate in the interest of national security as the government claims. It is far more likely that they will be used to curb dissent" (Sivapalan and Sabhaney 2019).

The Erosion of Democratic Values

In multicultural nation-states, the State is often presented as taking a "culture-blind" approach, while in reality, the values of the State are simply an embodiment of the culture of the majority, pushing aside minority cultures. This "culture-blind" strategy proves deadly to groups whose values are strictly opposed to the majority culture, often culminating in discrimination, repression, and—in the worst cases—genocide and forced assimilation. Minority communities are often sidelined in favor of adopting a "common vision" for the nation in an attempt to appear united and homogenous. As previously mentioned, the very preamble of the Indian Constitution vows to uphold a "sovereign socialist secular democratic republic," with guarantees of justice, liberty, and equality for all. However, in the 21st century, it is clear that for nearly all communities but middle and upper-caste Hindus, the Indian government has failed miserably in its pathetic attempt to sustain these assurances. Patwant Singh notes that "in a number of 'democracies' around the world today, just representation in the upper echelons of government is a rare thing; religious, caste, and class considerations matter far more" (Singh and Rai 2008, 116). Ranjit Singh's monarchical government was more in keeping with democratic and secular principles than the flawed and broken democracy in India today. While the Constitution contains promises of religious, economic, social, and political freedoms, these promises have yet to be realized in any meaningful capacity, particularly in the case of the Sikh community. Of the 195 officially recognized UN states, India consistently ranks abysmally low in independent freedom ranking reports.

Ronald Inglehart argues that a common interpretation is that democratic institutions inherently make people happy, healthy, tolerant, and trusting, and that democracy instills post-materialist values. While this interpretation is extremely appealing and provides a powerful argument for democracy while implying a quick fix for most of the world's problems, the experience of the Sikhs in India and minority groups around the world does not support this interpretation. Democracy, while an extremely valuable and integral institution, is not a magic wand. Since the Soviet Union's shift toward democracy (albeit a dangerously flawed and poorly implemented one) in 1991, the country has not become significantly healthier, happier, more trusting, more tolerant, or more post-materialist. Rather, it can be argued they have gone in the exact opposite direction. Another example of this can be found in Latin America's history of constitutional instability. Similarly in India, the experience of the Indian people does not support the argument for democracy being a quick solution—rather, an examination of extreme cultural and religious divisions must be taken into account when implementing a democracy to ensure the fair representation of all parties. While democracy can be a powerful and uplifting foundation to a country, its implementation must take into context the historical demographic differences within the population. India, a nation aspiring to rank among the world's leaders, has long remained in dire straits regarding human and democratic rights, according to even its own development experts. Its population has surpassed one billion and is on track to overtake China for its role as the most populous nation. However, statistics regarding the disadvantaged of India are glaring: barely half of India's population is literate—a common indicator of a fully productive society (Crossette and Harrison 2000, 183).

A free society in political terms does not necessarily result in a better life, as more than 100 million poor, illiterate, and often victimized women in India could demonstrate. Currently, little more than a third of the nation's women are able to read and write (Crossette and Harrison 2000, 182). Up to half of the births are not registered, making it difficult for millions of children to access basic services. Furthermore, development studies report that the broader social indicators in India are pulling the South Asian region down to or below the level of sub-Saharan Africa (ibid). The problems are most acute in northern India, where UNICEF reports that no women are literate in many villages in the state of Bihar (Crossette and Harrison 2000, 182). Nationwide, half of India's children are malnourished, with nearly one in five affected to the point of stunted growth. Twenty percent of children under the age of five are severely underweight, less than 30 percent of the population has access to sanitation, and 20 percent of the population lacks clean water. India's northern states constitute a large percentage of these statistics. As gaps in the living standard grow and resources shrink, social unrest becomes increasingly inevitable.

India's "secularism" as defined in the Indian constitution, has also proven to be ideologically different from the Western model; while the West employs a "wall of separation" of the church and state, the secular ideal of India is expressed in the motto "Sarva Dharma Sambhava," or "Let Religions Prosper." As a result, the Indian government has not stayed out of the business of religion, and, because Hindus comprise over 83 percent of the country and dominate the political government posts, minority communities such as the Sikhs are sidelined and often explicitly targeted due to their unique identity and cultural values. Thus the government reinforces the idea of "encapsulation" of various minority groups, as the domination of an even-handed system by the majority inevitably leads to conflict and the degradation of human rights, lending credence to the fear that the "democracy" could slide into outright Hindu theocracy. Consequently, P.C. Upadyay refers to Indian "secularism" as "majoritarianism" (Mahmood 1997, 118). When Hindu nationalists advocate for the Hindu nation and synonymize being Indian and being Hindu, those who do not wish to sacrifice their cultural values and identity find themselves labeled as traitors, terrorists, and separatists, and their very culture attacked and annihilated.

While the Indian government and its supporters are eager to highlight India's status as the world's largest democracy, studies have observed trends indicating a deterioration of India's democratic standing. In its 2021 report *Democracy Under Siege*, the US-based non-profit, non-governmental Freedom House, which conducts research on political freedom and human rights, designated India, among other countries, as not free. Freedom House reported the "15th consecutive year of decline in global freedom," highlighting a deepening democratic recession. India, the "world's largest democracy," dropped from "Free" to "Partly Free" as Prime Minister Narendra Modi's administration cracked down on critics of the government (Repucci and Slipowitz 2021, 1-2). The ruling Hindu nationalist movement and increasing extremism encouraged the scapegoating and persecution of minorities, who faced attacks from vigilante mobs.

Additionally, in the case of the 2020 farmers' protests, which included a strike involving over 250 million people, the government's response was a clear indicator of India's negligence in its duty to democracy as the Modi administration arrested and prosecuted demonstrators, passed newly restrictive laws, and resorted to brutal crackdowns, for which they faced few international repercussions (Joy 2020). The Freedom Report continues, "With India's decline to "Partly Free", less than 20 percent of the world's population now lives in a "Free" country, the smallest proportion since 1995 (Repucci and Slipowitz 2021, 2). As repression intensifies in already unfree environments, greater damage is done to their institutions and societies, making it increasingly difficult to fulfill public demands for freedom and prosperity under any future government.

Considering India's massive population—over 1.37 billion people—Freedom House argues that India's decline from the list of free nations could have a rippling, damaging impact on global democratic standards. Due to India's standing as the second most populous nation and the 7th largest by geographic area, it is critical that India maintain and elevate its democracy; failure to do so could result in the destruction of democratic institutions throughout the entire world. Freedom House reports that "political rights and civil liberties in the country have deteriorated since Narendra Modi became prime minister in 2014, with increased pressure on human rights organizations, rising intimidation of academics and journalists, and a spate of bigoted attacks, including lynchings, aimed at Muslims" (Repucci and Slipowitz 2021, 2). It appears that under Modi, India has abandoned its potential to serve as a global democratic leader, instead choosing to prioritize Hindu nationalism at the expense of its original guarantees of secularism, inclusion, and "brotherhood". The Freedom House report concludes that "rather than serving as a champion of democratic practice and a counterweight to authoritarian influence from countries such as China, Modi, and his party are tragically driving India itself toward authoritarianism" (Repucci and Slipowitz 2021, 1).

Similarly, the Varieties of Democracy Institute (V-Dem), an independent Swedish-based research facility, classified India as an "electoral-autocracy," downgraded from a democracy, nearly doubling the total population living under autocracies. The V-Dem Institute's unique approach to calculating democracy using historical, multidimensional, and disaggregated data produced the largest global dataset on democracy for 202 countries from 1789 to the present day. In its 2021 report, *Autocratization Turns Viral,* V-Dem detailed India's gradual deterioration of freedom through the destruction of the media, academia, and civil society, which were curtailed first and most severely (Alizada et al 2021, 20). Out of 197 countries, India ranked 97th on the liberal democracy index, and 101st on the electoral democracy index; it also accounted for one of the top 10 largest decliners in freedoms. India's complete departure from its founding principles in favor of extreme right-wing Hindu nationalism has already exhibited international impacts and will continue to destroy democratic values even outside of its borders.

Additionally, the CATO Institute, another non-governmental think tank, recorded another decrease in freedoms in the annual *Human Freedom Index* report. Using over 76 independent variables of personal and economic freedom in a dozen areas on a scale of 0 to 10, CATO ranked India 111th out of 162 countries in 2019, a drop of 5 ranks from the previous 2018 report (Vásquez and McMahon 2020, 7). As shown in the graphics below, India's standing in human and economic freedoms has been stagnating and decreasing over the years—a dangerous sign for the largest aspiring "democracy" in the world. The Fraser Institute also noted a decline in India's economic freedoms, concluding that the data suggest "that economic freedom falls with population across... 17 Indian states" (Sobel 2021, 35). While India holds the potential to become a global economic power, corruption and its longtime adherence to archaic institutions such as the caste system have hindered its development.

Infographic from CATO *Human Freedom Index 2019* Report

Infographic from CATO *Human Freedom Index 2020* Report

Since its Independence, India has been able to maintain its standing as a democratic country embracing Western ideals. As Barbara Crosette notes in her portrait of the nation, the images of Gandhian pacifism and Eastern mysticism upheld by the Indian media-propaganda apparatus cover up a multitude of abuses both within and without India, keeping the world ignorant of the disaffection of the populace and erosion of democracy by the government (Crosette 1993). She notes that more Indian citizens fall victim to their own military and police each year than were killed during the entirety of the seventeen-year dictatorship of Augusto Pinochet of Chile. However, it is interesting to note that despite the intense levels of state-sponsored violence, mass protests within India have been scarce and international condemnation has been nonexistent. The "mantra" of democracy, as Crosette dubs it, overwhelms all dissenting voices.

For the Sikhs, the classification of the Indian State as undemocratic through various metrics is hardly surprising and only confirms what the community already understood, especially following the 1984 attacks. For minority groups, India has become little more than a country of neofascism fueled by reactionary political actors. While claiming to stand for democracy and secularism, the nation's actions reflect those of a majoritarian state. As Perry Anderson notes, "hidden within India is Hindustan. It is that which tacitly shapes the state and determines the frontiers between freedom and repression, what is allowed and what is forbidden" (Anderson 2013, 149). Over the years, it has become clear that the broader Hindu community seeks to define Sikhism, and is adamant that Sikhs should accept the definition and narrative set by the Hindu elite.

Huntington argues that the world is divided into approximately nine major civilizations based on centuries-long cultural differences, and that future conflicts will occur largely along these cultural fault lines. These civilizations are largely defined by religious influences that, despite forces of modernization, continue to remain powerful (Inglehart and Harrison 2000, 81). Today, the contrast between "Operation Blue Star" and "genocide" as two different perceptions of the same reality is symptomatic of the wide gap between the story told by the Indian government and the Sikh community's recollection of the events at the Golden Temple when the army attacked in June 1984. Since then, the government has continued to oppress the people of Punjab, exercising extreme levels of authoritarian action under the unsubstantiated justifications of counter-terrorism. The Hindu-led Indian state alone decides whether its resources will be used to educate and support the people of Punjab or to surveil them. Invading their lives and swamping the airwaves with nationalist movies promoting unity while ignoring historical facts, besieging the markets, controlling the merest resources, initiatives, and potentialities, India has hindered the Sikh community from the birth of the country. Most recently, in October of 2021, the central government issued an order increasing the jurisdiction of the Border Security Force in India, granting its officers the power to arrest, search, and seize anywhere within 50 km of the Punjab border. Earlier, this range was 15 km (The Tribune India 2021). This puts over half (27,650 square kilometers out of 50,362 square kilometers) of Punjab's territory under Central government authority.

The story of the Sikh community has been, and always will be one of disproportionality. From its very inception, the Sikh faith has repeatedly run contrary to the establishment faiths of its time and geography, namely: Hinduism, Islam, and Buddhism. However, the culture and institutions developed over 238 years by the Sikh Gurus and maintained by the Sikh leaders continue to serve as a source of guidance and unity for the community. As Patwant Singh states, "the resilience and ruggedness of the Sikh faith and its followers, and their resolve and spirit of independence, were and are continuously nurtured by the Guru Granth Sahib and its evocative, balanced, rational and realistic view of life. It has sustained the Sikhs in the past and will continue to do so in the future" (Singh and Rai 2008, 284). Indeed, the Indian state's attack on the Golden Temple openly demonstrated that which had lurked in the shadows since Independence: a nefarious desire to crush and destroy the Sikh community while promoting a dangerous Hindu nationalist ideology. Since then, the Indian government, through its state-sanctioned media and outward support of Hindu extremist groups, has vilified any Sikh who dares raise a voice against the government. At this stage, it is clear that the cultural differences between the two groups and the extensive history of oppression and conflict present themselves as obstacles in the way of democracy that are unlikely to be overcome without radical changes.

The Indian government's utter failure in upholding democracy in a nation of 1.4 billion should serve as a dire warning to the Sikhs that their rights are and shall continue to be violated until they form and maintain a more autonomous Punjab or completely separate Sikh nation. The Sikh experience over the centuries demonstrates genocides can only be prevented or disrupted through the ascension of political power; in the absence of political and military authority, minority cultures and civilizations are under threat of extermination from those who rule. Since the fall of the Sikh Empire on the 29th of March, 1849, the Sikh cultural values and institutional powers have been diminished. This phenomenon is unsurprising considering the duration for which intense political forces have attempted to suppress the faith—with Sikhs themselves falling victim to government propaganda. If further genocide is to be prevented, Sikh leaders must awake from the spell of Stockholm Syndrome that has entrapped the community and develop a strategy to provide leadership to the Sikhs, making them aware of what they were, what they are, and what they are supposed to be.

BIBLIOGRAPHY

Bibliography

Alizada, Nazifa, Rowan Cole, Lisa Gastaldi, Sandra Grahn, Sebastian Hellmeier, Palina Kolvani, Jean Lachapelle, Anna Lührmann, Seraphine F. Maerz, Shreeya Pillai. 2021. *Autocratization Turns Viral: Democracy Report 2021.* Gothernberg, Sweden: V-Dem Institute at the University of Gothenburg.

Althusser, Louis. 2001. *Lenin and Philosophy, and other Essays.* Translated by Ben Brewster. New York: Monthly Review Press.

Anderson, Benedict. 2016. *Imagined Communities: Reflections on the Origin and Spread of Nationalism.* London: Verso.

Anderson, Perry. 2013. *The Indian Ideology.* London: Verso.

Amnesty International. 1995. *India: Punjab Police; Beyond the Bounds of the Law.* Amnesty International: International Secretariat.

Barr, William. 1844. *Journal of a March from Delhi to Peshawur and from Thence to Cabul with the Mission of Lieutenant Colonel Sir C.M. Wade Kt CB.* London: James Madden.

Bhatia, Sardar Singh. 1998. "Vadda Ghallughara." In *The Encyclopedia of Sikhism.* Volume IV.
Patiala: Punjabi University.

Bhangu, Rattan Singh, and Vir Singh. 1993. *Panth Prakash*. Delhi: Bhai Vir Singh Sahitya Sadan.

Bose, Sugata, and Ayesha Jalal. 2018. *Modern South Asia: History, Culture, Political Economy*. New York: Routledge.

Boswell, James. 1923. *Life of Samuel Johnson*. New York: Scott, Foresman, & Company.

Brass, Paul R. 2015. *Production of Hindu-Muslim Violence in Contemporary India*. Seattle: University of Washington Press.

Crossette, Barbara and Lawrence E. Harrison. 2000. *Culture Matters: How Values Shape Human Progress. IV: Culture and Gender*. New York: Basic Books.

Crossette, Barbara. 1993. *India: Facing the Twenty-First Century*. Bloomington: Indiana University Press.

Cunningham, Joseph Davey. 1966 [1849]. *A History of the Sikhs: From The Origin of the Nation to the Battles of the Sutlej*. London: J. Murray.

Darshi, A. R. 2004. *The Gallant Defender*. Ludhiana: Jaswant Printers.

Deol, Harnik. 2000. *Religion and Nationalism in India: The Case of the Punjab*. New York: Routledge.

Dev, Atul. 2019. "India's Supreme Court Is Teetering on the Edge". The Atlantic. April 28, 2019. https://www.theatlantic.com /international/archive/2019/04/india-supreme-court-corruption/587152/

Dhillon, Gurdarshan Singh. 1974. "Evolution Of The Demand For A Sikh Homeland." *The Indian Journal Of Political Science*, Vol. 35, No. 4.

Dhillon, Gurdarshan Singh. 1996. "Truth about Punjab: SGPC White Paper (1st ed.)" Amritsar, Punjab: Shiromani Gurdwara Parbandhak Committee.

Dhillon, Kirpal S. 2006. *Identity and Survival: Sikh Militancy in India, 1978-1993*. London: Penguin Books.

Duggal, Kartar Singh. 2001. *Maharaja Ranjit Singh: The Last to Lay Arms*. New Delhi: Abhinav Publications.

Dumont, Louis. 1970. *Homo Hierarchicus: An Essay on the Caste System*. Chicago: University of Chicago Press.

Duschinski, Haley, Mona Bhan, Ather Zia, and Cynthia Mahmood. 2018. *Resisting Occupation in Kashmir*. Philadelphia: University of Pennsylvania Press.

Embree, Ainslie T. 2018. *Utopias In Conflict: Religion And Nationalism in Modern India*. Berkeley: University Of California Press.

Etounga-Manguelle, Daniel and Lawrence E. Harrison. 2000. *Culture Matters: How Values Shape Human Progress. IV: Culture and Gender*. New York: Basic Books.

Gandhi, Mahatma. 1989. *The Collected Works of Mahatma Gandhi*. Vol. 28. New Delhi: Publications Division, Ministry of Information and Broadcasting, Government Of India.

Gramsci, Antonio. 1971. *Selections from the Prison Notebooks*. New York: International Publishers.

Green, Linda. 1994. "Fear as a Way of Life." *Cultural Anthropology* 9, no. 2 (1994): 227–56.

Grewal, J. S. 1998. *The Sikhs of the Punjab*. Cambridge: Cambridge University Press.

Hajari, Nisid. 2016. Midnight's Furies: The Deadly Legacy Of India's Partition. Boston: Houghton Mifflin Harcourt.

Hansen, Thomas Blom. 2008. "The Political Theology of Violence in Contemporary India", South Asia Multidisciplinary Academic Journal [Online]. http://journals.openedition.org /samaj/1872

Hugel, Karl Alexander, and D. C. Sharma. 1984. *Kashmir under Maharaja Ranjit Singh: Its Artistic Products, Taxation System, Imports & Exports, and Trade*. New Delhi: Atlantic.

Hugel, Karl Alexander, and T. B. Jervis. 1845. *Travels in Kashmir and the Panjab*. Cambridge: Cambridge University Press.

Huntington, Samuel. 1996. *The Clash of Civilizations and the Remaking of World Order*. New York: Simon & Schuster.

Huntington, Samuel P and Lawrence E. Harrison. 2000. *Culture Matters: How Values Shape Human Progress. Foreword: Cultures Count*. New York: Basic Books.

Inglehart, Robert and Lawrence E. Harrison. 2000. *Culture Matters: How Values Shape Human Progress. IV: Culture and Gender*. New York: Basic Books.

Jaffrelot, Christophe. 1996. *The Hindu Nationalist Movement in India*. New York: Columbia University Press.

Jaijee, Inderjit Singh. 1999. *Politics of Genocide: Punjab, 1984-1998*. Delhi: Ajanta Publications.

Jawandha, Nahar Singh. 2010. *Glimpses Of Sikhism*. New Delhi: Sanbun Publisher.

Joshi, Chand. 1984. *Bhindranwale: Myth and Reality*. New Delhi: Vikas.

Joy, Shemin. 2020. "At Least 25 Crore Workers Participated in General Strike; Some States Saw Complete Shutdown: Trade Unions." Deccan Herald. November 26, 2020. https://www.deccanherald.com/national/at-least-25-crore-workers-participated-in-general-strike-some-states-saw-complete-shutdown-trade-unions-920200.html

Kashmeri, Zuhair, and Brian McAndrew. 1989. *Soft Target: How the Indian Intelligence Service Penetrated Canada*. Toronto: J. Lorimer.

Katherine, Adeney and Lawrence Sáez, eds. 2015. *Coalition Politics and Hindu Nationalism*. New York: Routledge.

Khilnani, Sunil. 2007. "Nehru's Faith." In *The Crisis of Secularism in India*. Edited by Anuradha Dingwaney Needham and Rajeswari Sunder Rajan, 89-103. Ranikhet: Permanent Black.

Lawrence, Henry Montgomery. 1970. *Adventures of an Officer in the Punjab*. Patiala: Languages Department, Punjab University.

Lindsay, Stace and Lawrence E. Harrison. 2000. *Culture Matters: How Values Shape Human Progress. XXI: Culture, Mental Models, and National Prosperity.* New York: Basic Books.

Macauliffe, Max Arthur. 1909. *The Sikh Religion, Its Gurus, Sacred Writings And Authors.* In 6 Volumes. Oxford: At the Clarendon Press.

"The MacNeil/Lehrer NewsHour," 1984. Boston and Washington, DC: NewsHour Productions, American Archive of Public Broadcasting (GBH and the Library of Congress). June 4, 1984. http://americanarchive.org/catalog/cpb-aacip -507-nc5s757b0s

Mahmood, Cynthia Keppley. 1997. *Fighting for Faith and Nation: Dialogues with Sikh Militants.* Philadelphia: University of Pennsylvania Press.

Mahmood, Cynthia Keppley. 1989. "Sikh Rebellion and the Hindu Concept of Order." Asian Survey, Vol. 29, No. 3: 326–40.

Mookherjee, Nayanika. 2015. *The Spectral Wound: Sexual Violence, Public Memories, and the Bangladesh War of 1971.* Durham: Duke University Press.

Mukhoty, Gobinda and Rajni Kothari. 1984. "Who Are The Guilty?" *Outlook India.*

Nanavati, G.T. 2005. *1984 Anti-Sikh Reports.* Volume I. New Delhi, India: Justice Nanavati Commission Of Inquiry, 2005. https://www.mha.gov.in/sites/default/files/Nanavati-I_eng_0.pdf

Nijjar, Bakhshish Singh. 1995. "Chhota Ghallughara'', The Encyclopedia Of Sikhism, Volume I. Patiala: Punjabi University: 460–61.

Pande, B.D. 2021. *In the Service of Free India: Memoir of a Civil Servant.* New Delhi: Speaking Tiger Books.

Perkins, C. Ryan. n.d. "1947 Partition of India & Pakistan." Accessed 7 April 20, 2022. https://exhibits.stanford.edu/1947-partition/about/1947-partition-of-india-pakistan.

Pettigrew, Joyce. 1995. *The Sikhs of the Punjab: Unheard Voices of State and Guerilla Violence.* Atlantic Highlands, N.J.: Zed Books.

Pillalamarri, Akhilesh. 2014. "India's Anti-Sikh Riots 30 Years On". *The Diplomat.* October 31, 2014. https://thediplomat.com/2014/10/indias-anti-sikh-riots-30-years-on/

Rao, Amiya. 1986. *Oppression in Punjab: A Citizens for Democracy Report to the Nation.* Southall: Sikh Human Rights Group.

Repucci, Sarah and Amy Slipowitz. 2021. *Democracy under Siege.* Washington, DC: Freedom House. https://freedomhouse.org/sites/default/files/2021-03/FIW2021_Abridged_03112021_FINAL.pdf

Roy, Kaushik. 2011. *War, Culture, and Society in Early Modern South Asia, 1740-1849.* Oxon: Routledge.

Sagoo, Harbans Kaur. 2001. *Banda Singh Bahadur and Sikh Sovereignty.* New Delhi: Deep & Deep Publications.

Sathananthan, S.M., K.T. Lalwani, S. Raghunath Iyengar, G. P. Mansukhani, Asha Bhatnagar, V. S. Godbole, and Hukham Singh. 1983. "Hindu-Sikh Conflict in Punjab: Causes and Cure (Report)." London: *Transatlantic India Times*.

Sapir, Edward. 1929. "The Status of Linguistics as a Science", *Language*, 5 (4): 207–214

Saikia, Yasmin. 2011. "War As History, Humanity In Violence: Women, Men And Memories Of 1971, East Pakistan/Bangladesh." In *Sexual Violence In Conflict Zones: From The Ancient World To The Era Of Human Rights*, edited by Elizabeth D. Heineman, 152-170. Philadelphia: University Of Pennsylvania Press.

Sandhu, Ranbir Singh. 1999. *Struggle for Justice: Speeches and Conversations of Sant Jarnail Singh Khalsa Bhindranwale*. Dublin, Ohio: Sikh Educational & Religious Foundation.

Seetal, Sohan Singh. 1971. *Rise of the Sikh Power and Maharaja Ranjeet Singh*. Punjab, India: Dhanpat Rai & Sons.

Shani, Giorgio. 2008. *Sikh Nationalism and Identity in a Global Age*. London: Routledge.

Shrivastava, Aseem. 2005. "The Winter In Delhi 1984". *Counterpunch*. https://www.counterpunch.org/2005/12/10/the-winter-in-delhi-1984/.

Sidiq, Nusra. 2020. "Kashmir Shuts Down to Mark Afzal Guru Death Anniversary." *Anadolu Agency*.

Sikh Federation (UK). 2007."Written evidence submitted by the Sikh Federation (UK)." UK House of Commons: Select Committee on Foreign Affairs. 18 April 2007.

Sikh Press Associates. 2019. "Know the Facts of 1984 Sikh Genocide." May 29, 2019. https://www.sikhpa.com/know-the-facts-of-1984-sikh-genocide

Singh Ganda, Banda Singh Bahadur, Bhai Sahib Bhai Vir Singh ji, and Sardar Bahadur S. Bishen Singh. 1935. *Life of Banda Singh Bahadur*. Amritsar: Sikh History Research Department.

Singh, Gurnam. 1960. *A Unilingual Punjabi State and the Sikh Unrest: A Statement*. New Delhi: Super Press.

Singh, Kapur. 1966. *Betrayal of the Sikhs*. Delhi: Akali Dal.

Singh, Khushwant. 1978. *A History of the Sikhs. Volume I: 1469–1839*. Delhi, Oxford University Press.

Singh, Teja and Kohli, Sita Ram. 1986. *Maharaja Ranjit Singh*. New Delhi: Atlantic Publishers.

Singh, Gurmit. 1989. *History of Sikh Struggles*. Vol 1. New Delhi: Atlantic Publishers & Distributors.

Santokh Singh. 1994. *Sri Suraj Prakash: Jiwan Britant Das Patshahian*. Amritsar: Chattar Singh Jiwan Singh.

Singh, Major Gurmukh (retd). 1997. *Sant Jarnail Singh Bhindrānvāle*. Edited by Harbans Singh. Patiala, Punjab: Punjab University.

Singh Daljeet, Kharak Singh, and Choor Singh Sidhu. 1997. *Sikhism: Its Philosophy and History*. Chandigarh: Institute of Sikh Studies.

Singh, Bhagat. 1998. *The Encyclopedia Of Sikhism*. Volume IV. Patiala: Punjabi University.

Singh, Patwant, and Jyoti M. Rai. 2008. *Empire of the Sikhs: The Life and Times of Maharaja Ranjit Singh*. New Delhi, India: Hay House India.

Singh, Ajmer. 2009. *1984: Unchitviya Kehar*. Amritsar: Singh Brothers.

Singh, Guru Gobind. 2011. *Zafarnama*. Translated by Sarna, Navtej. New Delhi, India: Penguin Books India.

Singh, Sangat. 2014. *The Sikhs in History*. Amritsar: Singh Brothers.

Singh, Sirdar Kapur. 2016. "The Golden Temple | Sirdar Kapur Singh | Sikhri Articles." *Sikhri.org*. April 25, 2016. https://sikhri.org/articles/the-golden-temple-its-theo-political-status.

Sivapalan, Bhamati and Vidyun Sabhaney. 2019. "From Colonial Era to Today's India, a Visual History of National Security Laws Used to Crush Dissent." August 24, 2019. https://scroll.in/article/930973/from-colonial-era-to-todays-india-a-visual-history-of-national-security-laws-used-to-crush-dissent.

Sobel, Russel S. 2021. *The Determinants of Subnational Economic Freedom: An Analysis of Data for Seven Countries With Implications for Optimal Jurisdiction Size*. Fraser Institute.

Stepan, Alfred, Yogendra Yadav, and Juan Linz. 2012. *Crafting State-nations: India and Other Multinational Democracies.* Baltimore: Johns Hopkins University Press.

Stevens, William. 1984. "Punjab Raid: Unanswered Questions." *The News York Times*, 19 June 1984.

Thali, Jagdeep Singh. 1984. *D5 Channel Punjabi.* Youtube. June 1984. https://www.youtube.com /watch?v=3w_X7g2RdiE&ab_channel=D5ChannelPunjabi

Telford, Hamish. 1992.. "The Political Economy of Punjab: Creating Space for Sikh Militancy". *Asian Survey.* 46 (11): 969–987.

Thukral, Gobind. 1982. "What Kind of Man Is Sant Jarnail Singh Bhindranwale?" *India Today*, 30 April 1982.

The Tribune India. 2019. "AFDR Regrets Life Term to Three Youths". February 10, 2019. https://www.tribuneindia.com /news/archive/bathinda/afdr-regrets-life-term-to-three-youths-727233

The Tribune India. 2021. "BSF Can Now Conduct Raids, Make Seizures Up to 50 Km From Border." https://www.tribuneindia.com/news/nation/bsf-can-now-conduct-raids-make-seizures-up-to-50-km-from-border-324242

Trivedi, Upmanyu. 2021. "Even India's Ex-Chief Justice Won't Go to Nation's Courts". *Bloomberg Quint.* February 11, 2021. https://www.bloombergquint.com/law-and-policy/india-ex-top-judge-won-t-seek-justice-from-ramshackled-courts

Tuli, Pritpal Singh, and Jatinder Kumar. 2015. *Walking With The Gurus*. B. Chattar Singh Jiwan Singh: Amritsar, India.

Van Dyke, Virginia. 1996. "The Anti-Sikh Riots of 1984 in Delhi: Politicians, Criminals, and the Discourse of Communalism." In *Riots and Pogroms*, edited by Paul Brass, 201-220. London: Palgrave Macmillan UK.

Vásquez, Ian and Fred McMahon. 2020. *The Human Freedom Index 2020: A Global Measurement of Personal, Civil, and Economic Freedom*. Washington, DC: Cato Institute and the Fraser Institute.

Verma, Dr. S.S. 2021. "Education In The Times Of Maharaja Ranjit Singh Ji". *Scind.Org*. https://scind.org/article/Education-in-the-times-of-Maharaja-RANJIT-SINGH-ji.

Voice Online. 2014. "Los Angeles Court Summons Amitabh Bachchan for Raising Slogan 'Khoon Ka Badla Khoon' in 1984 Sikh 'Genocide." *Voice Online*. October 29, 2014, https://voiceonline.com/los-angeles-court-summons-amitabh-bachchan-for-raising-slogan-khoon-ka-badla-khoon-in-1984-sikh-genocide/

Weaver, Mary Anne. 1984. "India's Sikhs Are Bitter As Army Tries To Weed Out 'Militants.'" *The Christian Science Monitor*. October 15, 1984. https://www.csmonitor.com /1984/1015/101540.html. Weber, Eugen. 2007. *Peasants into Frenchmen: The Modernization of Rural France, 1870-1914*. Stanford: Stanford University Press.

Weber, Max. 2013. *Economy and Society: An Outline of Interpretive Sociology*. Volume 1. Edited by Guenther Roth and Claus Wittich. Berkeley: University Of California Press.

ABOOKS

ALIVE Book Publishing and ALIVE Publishing Group
are imprints of Advanced Publishing LLC,
3200 A Danville Blvd., Suite 204, Alamo, California 94507

Telephone: 925.837.7303
alivebookpublishing.com